Preserved
Steam Locomotives
of Britain

Preserved
Steam Locomotives
of Britain

Colin Garratt

BLANDFORD PRESS

POOLE   DORSET

First published in the U.K. 1982 by
Blandford Press, Link House, West Street,
Poole, Dorset, BH15 1LL

Copyright © 1982 Blandford Books Ltd.

British Library Cataloguing in Publication Data

Garratt, Colin
   Preserved steam locomotives of Britain. –
   (Colour series)
   1. Locomotives – Great Britain – History
   I. Title
   625.2'6'0941   TJ603.4G7

ISBN 0 7137 0917 0

Typeset in 10/11½ pt Monophoto Ehrhardt
by Oliver Burridge and Co. Ltd.
Printed in Singapore by
Toppan Printing Co. (S) Pte. Ltd.

Contents

Colour Plate List

The Colour Plates appear on pages 65 to 96.

8

Introduction

This book is intended to be a companion volume to *Preserved Steam Railways of Britain* (Blandford Press, 1978) which, as a travel guide, highlighted the many working preserved lines and static locomotive collections around the country. In this volume I have endeavoured to place into perspective the vast array of preserved locomotive types which can be found at these establishments.

Almost without exception, Britain's preserved steam centres hold a disparate and random selection of locomotives which seldom bear any relationship to each other, or to their place in locomotive evolution. Inevitably, such a situation presents confusion to all but the few blessed with a broad knowledge of locomotive history, and the following pages are intended to break down any such ambiguities by categorising the locomotives into seven basic 'orders' which relate directly to the purpose for which the engines were created: Industrial, Goods, Express Passenger, Narrow Gauge, Shunting, Suburban and Mixed Traffic. These orders are set in evolutionary sequence—*i.e.* Britain's first steam locomotive was an industrial, and the last and most sophisticated were mixed-traffics.

Usually, the order to which a locomotive belongs is easily defined, but the reader will detect instances of certain types straddling two different orders. One example of this is the pre-nationalisation suburban/branch line engines which were actually designated mixed-traffics. In this instance, I have grouped the engines in relation to what they actually did; but as far as the British Railway's standards are concerned, I have conceded that the evolution towards the mixed traffic concept was largely complete, and grouped the engines accordingly.

Cross-fertilisation of orders occurs with many engines and instances are highlighted throughout the book. One example concerns old goods engines being downgraded as shunters, so moving from one order to another. However, in evolutionary terms they are goods engines, as this was their *raison d'être*.

Continuing the analogy with the natural sciences, orders break down into 'families', 'genera', 'species' and 'sub-species'. I define a family of locomotives within a given order as those of a particular wheel arrangement *i.e.* in the Mixed Traffic order the 2-6-0—or Mogul—represents a family of engines. These families consist of genera which are made up of groups of engines with common characteristics, and to cite the Moguls once again, a typical genus would consist of those designed or influenced by Gresley—Classes K1, K2, K3 and K4. The species (or the class, in popular locomotive terminology) is, of course, the individual design, whilst sub-species embraces any tangible variations which were made upon it: a perfect example here is the Great Western Hall as the species and the Modified Hall—as built from 1944 onwards—as the sub-species.

By applying such a system of classification, the observer can quickly evaluate an individual locomotive's place within the evolutionary scale. This knowledge can either be used as a springboard from which to delve further into Britain's gloriously rich locomotive heritage, or simply as the basis for greater appreciation of the locomotives which can still be enjoyed today.

In conclusion, I am indebted to the photographers who have contributed many fine pictures to this book, and also to Roger Crombleholme who, apart from helping to collate the illustrations, has made many valuable suggestions towards the book as a whole. Finally, I thank my mother for typing the manuscript so assiduously.

Colin Garratt,
Newton Harcourt,
1982.

SECTION 1

Locomotives of Industry

The world's first steam locomotive was born on the South Wales coalfield in 1804 and until the advent of the main line railway twenty-one years later, all engines built were for colliery service. These early engines bore little generic resemblance to the industrial steam locomotive as we know it today; they were disparate in kind and often unsuccessful, but some did manage to take the place of horses on the colliery wagonways. Early industrial engines had reached Yorkshire by 1812 and a few years later they appeared on the Northumberland coalfield.

The advent of main line railways from 1825 onwards provided an unprecedented boost to the industrial revolution. The steam locomotive had evolved to a reliable state of development, and the networks spread across the country with incredible rapidity. It became possible to transport vital goods and minerals in quantities which were unimaginable under the Canal System. By the 1840s the frenzied construction of lines had reached unprecedented proportions and was referred to as The Railway Mania.

Railway building was undertaken by contractors who employed huge gangs of navvies to construct the necessary cuttings, embankments, tunnels and viaducts. So vast was the scale of operation that contractors engines were demanded to supplement the muscle power of the navvies and horses. Initially, early main line engines were pensioned off into this type of service, as indeed they were to the collieries, but these proved unsuitable—a new order of locomotives had to evolve. The requirement was for a compact and economical engine light enough to work over poor tracks, able to negotiate tight curves and yet have sufficient adhesion to draw heavy trainloads of earth and materials. Furthermore, the engines needed to be easy to transport from one site to another; small tank engines were the obvious answer.

Commensurate with this great period of railway building came enormous demands for iron. Quarries and foundries developed side by

side, whilst the attendant need for coal meant new collieries being struck, combined with a better output from existing ones. Other aspects of heavy industry were developed as were docks and harbours, all of which had to be connected with the main railway network. These multifarious industrial activities also demanded locomotives of their own and the contractor's tank provided the ideal basis. Thus, by 1850 the industrial steam locomotive as we know it today had been born.

In contrast with its pristine ancestors, the definitive industrial engine evolved as either a side or saddle tank, four or six coupled. Saddle tanks were generally preferred, as apart from providing easy access to the motion, a tank hugging the engine's boiler permitted warming of the feed water. Side tanks on the other hand held more water, but tended to restrict access to the moving parts. All had two cylinders which ideally were placed inside the frame—partly to protect the moving rods from objects fouling the loading gauge, but also to provide lateral strength. However, the short boiler on many 0-4-0s provided insufficient room for a crankaxle, and the cylinders were placed outside. The 0-4-0 had the ability to negotiate tight

Above Left
Aveling Porter 2–2–0 of 1872 at Fawley Hill Railway. This early form of industrial engine was built by Aveling Porter of Rochester to convey chalk from the Kent pits. Aveling Porter were principally noted for their steam rollers and this engine is, in effect, a traction engine running on rails. Its single cylinder is attached to a fly wheel and set on top of the boiler. Though ideal for slow heavy hauling its development led to an evolutionary blind alley, and the type hardly spread beyond its native Kent. First introduced in 1865, building continued for sixty years in versions which ranged from four to twenty horsepower. The principle of adopting road practice to rail by means of low gearing was later taken up by Sentinel with much greater success, and when the last Aveling Porter was built in 1926 it was archaic and primitive.

Above
Andrew Barclay 0–4–0ST No. 1047 built in 1905 and preserved on the Stour Valley Railway, a typical example of the great Kilmarnock school as exemplified by Andrew Barclay, whose company commenced building 0–4–0STs in 1859; by the 1890s a highly characteristic shape had evolved which was perpetuated right through until the late 1950s in both four and six coupled form. Similar engines to the one shown were built with 12, 14, 15, and 16 in. diameter cylinders on various wheelbases, depending upon customer's needs. Unlike the other principal design schools, Barclays built no 18 in. cylinder 0–6–0ST, but reached this dimension with one of their few industrial Side Tank classes.

curves, and to go virtually anywhere that a wagon could. Accordingly such engines found favour in docks, ironworks, quarries, power stations and factories, whereas the 0-6-0s tended to be used in collieries and the larger mines.

During its evolution, the 0-4-0's cylinder sizes progressed from 7 in. diameter to 15 in., whilst the 0-6-0 ranged from 11 to 18 in. Driving wheel diameters were a mean 3 ft. on the 0-4-0 and 4 ft. on the 0-6-0, and whereas the smallest 0-4-0 weighed as little as 12 tons in full working order, the largest of the 0-6-0s topped 50 tons.

Infinite variations were played on these basic concepts with engines superficially identical in appearance having different cylinder sizes, wheelbases or even wheel arrangements. These variations characterise the entire evolution of the industrial locomotive, which, strange as it may seem, remained fundamentally unaltered over more than a century. This is at complete variance with the dramatic evolution of main line passenger engines—compare the *Rocket* of 1829 with an L.N.E.R. A4 of 1935! Obviously the industrial engine was limited by its environment but whatever rationalisations took place within the various industries, the engines simply grew in size on the same four and six-coupled wheelbases.

Although the locomotives varied little, several distinctive schools of design quickly established themselves. The first was based upon Leeds, which is regarded as the home of the industrial locomotive.

Above Right
Hudswell Clarke 0-6-0T *Nunlow* built in 1938 and preserved at the Dinting Railway Centre. The antecedents of this engine lie in a class of 0-6-0Ts built by Hudswell Clarke of Leeds for the Barry Port & Gwendraeth Valley Railway in 1909. This class represented a departure from tradition for Hudswell Clarke as, prior to its inception, the company had built to the old Railway Foundry coupled wheelbase of 10 ft. 9 in. in order to keep the valve gear drawings standard. The B.P.G.V. engines with their 13 ft. 7 in. wheelbase precipitated a new line of development in 0-6-0Ts and one which became a Hudswell Clarke standard for such industrial establishments as collieries and docks. Building of the type continued until 1955.

Right
Avonside 0-4-0ST No. 1875 built in 1921 and seen on the Colne Valley Railway. The engine typifies the Bristol family. She is a standard inside-cylinder 0-4-0ST built by Avonside and has a copper cap chimney, Ramsbottom safety valves mounted on her dome, a Peckett style flat sided smokebox and a 'Bristol' sandbox. She personifies the long line of attractive 0-4-0STs, built by the Bristol School.

Building began here in 1812 with the construction of the Blenkinsop Murray engine for the Middleton Colliery. This gave rise to the establishing of E. B. Wilson's Railway Foundry along with Kitsons & Co., both of which were located in the parish of Hunslet. Wilson's began building tank engines for contractors during the 1840s and when this company broke up in 1858, there emerged on the site Manning Wardle, the inheritors of E. B. Wilson's drawings, and Hudswell Clarke. Four years later, in the same parish, a company called J. T. Leather was formed, which in 1872 took the name of The Hunslet Engine Co. Thus, the parish of Hunslet had four major locomotive builders, and its traditions of building industrial engines made Leeds famous throughout the world. The Leeds school is generally associated with inside cylinder engines and its significance is demonstrated by over 150 locomotives in preservation today. Further south, in Sheffield the production of industrials was commenced during the 1860s by the Yorkshire Engine Company, who built a varied range of saddle tanks over a ninety year period. Only three have been preserved.

With Leeds established as the cradle of the industrial locomotive, production began elsewhere and the coal and iron industries of Ayrshire gave rise to the famous locomotive builders of Kilmarnock. This school dates from the 1870s and over the following eighty years, the town became noted for a highly distinctive family of 0-4-0 and 0-6-0 saddle tanks with outside cylinders. Several builders were involved, by far the most important being Andrew Barclay, but the works of Grant Ritchie and Dick Kerr were also significant. Apart from being extensively used in Scotland, Kilmarnock's engines saw service throughout the entire country. Over one hundred Kilmarnock engines remain under preservation.

Although Glasgow was of infinitely greater significance in locomotive building than Kilmarnock, it did not acquire so much eminence in the production of industrial engines, at least as far as the British market was concerned. Some noted types, however, were Neilson's 0-4-0ST 'Pugs' along with Sharp Stewart's family of saddle tanks.

As might be imagined, a locomotive building tradition began south of the border on Tyneside to serve the many collieries and ironworks in the area. Early builders in Newcastle were Black Hawthorn and R. &. W. Hawthorn, but it was not until 1884, when R. &. W. Hawthorn merged with A. Leslie (Shipbuilders) to form Hawthorn Leslie, that one of the most famous names in industrial locomotive history

Robert Stephenson & Hawthorn 0–4–0ST, *Sir Cecil A. Cochrane* built in 1948. The engine is depicted on the Tanfield Railway. Though built by Robert Stephenson & Hawthorn, this 0–4–0ST's design originated with Hawthorn Leslie during the early years of the century. It was a popular type with Electricity Works and was part of a progression of almost identical engines with cylinder diameters ranging from 10 to 14 in. This basic shape of engine symbolises the Newcastle Saddle Tank of the twentieth century, the 0–6–0s simply being an elongated version with a progression of larger cylinder sizes. Engines from this family were found in all aspects of British industry.

began. This company became noted for its range of outside cylinder four and six coupled saddle tanks, many of which were built with only detail variations for over half a century.

In 1937, Hawthorn Leslie merged with Robert Stephenson of Darlington to form Robert Stephenson & Hawthorn, and although building of the traditional Hawthorn Leslie designs continued, the amalgam also became known for its splendid 0–6–0 side tanks with 18 in. diameter cylinders, both builders having previously produced similar engines. These large side tanks were excellent for hauling heavy loads of coal to power stations from the main line sidings. In

addition, some large and highly potent saddle tanks were built for working in Northumberland collieries. Over seventy-five engines from the builders of the north-east have been preserved.

Within a few years of industrial engines being built on Tyneside, a tradition commenced in Bristol when Fox Walker began business in 1864. In 1880 this company was taken over by Thomas Peckett whose name was to become synonymous with superbly finished engines of considerable aesthetic merit. Peckett specialised mainly in small engines with a limited range. Bristol's other locomotive builder turned to the construction of industrial engines from 1889. This company, known as Avonside, was the descendant of Stothert Slaughter & Co., famous for building many broad gauge engines for the Great Western. Both Pecketts and Avonside built standard progressions of outside cylinder saddle tanks with a distinctly Bristol lineage. Both companies produced many engines for the industrialised areas of South Wales, where surprisingly no locomotive building tradition ever occurred. Over one hundred Bristol built engines are

Above Left
Andrew Barclay 0-4-0F built in 1956. This engine is depicted working at the Imperial Paper Mills, Gravesend, Kent. It has since been presented to the National Collection. The most important and successful variation ever played upon the industrial locomotive was the Fireless, which was built in four and six coupled form. The Fireless should still have relevance today, for it offers a pollution free engine which requires little maintenance and provides pleasant working conditions for its driver. Furthermore, the Fireless is not directly responsible for burning up valuable oil. However, although widely adopted, the Fireless family died out during the early 1960s as part of the national obsession to be rid of steam traction.

Left
Hunslet 16 in. 0-6-0ST *Ring Haw* at Nassington Ironstone Mines. This engine which was built in 1940 is now on the North Norfolk Railway. The Leeds built inside-cylinder 0-6-0ST represents one of the most noble lineages in British locomotive history. The type first appeared from the Railway Foundry, and many fine engines preceded this 16 in. design which was introduced by Hunslet in 1923. They were extremely powerful engines for their day, and heralded the advent of the big six-coupled tank in being a direct forerunner of the celebrated 18 in. Hunslet Austerities first introduced for wartime service in 1943. The Austerities continued to be built until 1964, by which time the class totalled 484 engines. They became the standard coalfield type under the N.C.B. although a few graduated into L.N.E.R. service as main line shunters. Before the last Austerity was built, some of the earlier engines had been withdrawn, a situation which renders them almost unique in world history. The Austerities also have the distinction of being the most numerous preserved class in the world, with over fifty engines saved.

preserved, including several which came from Fox Walker during the 1870s.

Having summarised the main areas of production, two other British towns must be mentioned—Stoke-upon-Trent with Kerr Stuart, and Stafford with Bagnalls. Both came to prevalence towards the end of the nineteenth century, and, although these firms produced many narrow gauge engines for contractors, estates and industry in general, large numbers of standard gauge engines were built, especially by Bagnalls. In all, fifty locomotives from this builder have been preserved, including two magnificent o-6-oSTs named *Vulcan* and *Victor* which heralded a new order of industrial locomotives. These engines were built during the steam versus diesel controversy of the 1950s, and the Steel Company of Wales invited Bagnalls to deliver both steam and diesel-electrics in order that a careful comparison might be made. This mandate stated that the steam engines were to be as advanced as possible and to incorporate every conceivable labour saving device. The result was three 18 in. o-6-oSTs with piston valves, outside Walschaerts valve gear, roller bearings, rocking grates, self cleaning smoke boxes and many other features totally new to the traditionally simple industrial saddle tank.

Peckett 0–6–0ST, works number 2000, built in 1942 and seen on the Nene Valley Railway. This lovely 0–6–0ST belongs to the Bristol School, and came from Pecketts in 1942. She is an example of a nineteenth century design, simply being enlarged to the requirements of the day. Even at this late date, Pecketts' traditional symmetry of design is in evidence.

Although industrial engines changed little during their century of pre-eminence, several significant variants did emerge, perhaps the most notable being the Fireless, a German innovation taken up by Andrew Barclay in 1913. Fireless engines take their steam second-hand from the work's boilers and constitute a low cost shunting unit for those industries with a ready supply of high pressure steam. Almost two hundred of these engines worked in Britain.

A totally different line of development was pursued by Sentinel of Shrewsbury who, from the 1920s onwards, built a family of geared industrials with vertical boilers. These engines represented a kind of halfway stage between steam and diesel, having been designed to utilise the full power of the boiler at any speed. Although the company claimed their engines effected huge savings in coal, oil and maintenance when compared with the conventional industrial locomotive, relatively few Sentinels appeared, but in common with the Fireless they are well represented under preservation.

Another innovation designed to prolong the life of steam came during the 1950s when Hunslet produced their Gas Producer System in which the locomotive consumed its own smoke. This was to comply with the Clean Air Act which was being rigidly imposed by many local authorities, especially as part of the drive to clean up the industrial north. Sadly, this splendid device could not save the steam locomotive and industrial users followed British Railway's policy of abandoning steam in favour of diesel traction. The keenly held theory that steam would survive in industry long after it vanished from the main lines proved not to be. Industrial locomotives preceded their main line counterparts by some twenty years, and survived them by approximately the same time span.

Preservationists have found the industrial engine cheaper to buy, easier to transport and less daunting to maintain than a main line locomotive. Paradoxically, many preserved industrials have been equipped with continuous braking gear for working passenger trains along preserved lines, a concept which would have been totally unimaginable to their builders. Over six hundred industrial engines— the products of some forty different builders—can be seen today in preserved form. This magnificent stud provides a fitting testimony to the key role the industrial steam locomotive played, for its period of pre-eminence coincided with Britain's historic lead as the premier industrial nation of the world.

SECTION 2

Goods Engines

When the steam locomotive emerged from the colliery tracks onto a main line in 1825, it did so in the form of an 0-4-0 tender type. The engine was *Locomotion*—the world's first goods engine—and the story of how she steamed along the Stockton & Darlington Railway hauling thirty-four wagons of coal is one of the classic tales in railway history.

Although *Locomotion* was relatively successful, the greater adhesion of a six coupled engine was felt to be preferable for hauling heavy loads. Consequently, in 1827-28 the railway received two 0-6-0s named *Victory* and *Experiment* which in common with *Locomotion* had been built at Robert Stephenson's newly formed works in Newcastle-upon-Tyne. With these historic locomotives, which had their roots in a colliery engine of 1816, the British 0-6-0 goods engine was born, albeit at this time with outside cylinders.

When the world's first passenger railway opened between Liverpool and Manchester in 1830, the locomotive chosen for the inauguration of the service was the famous *Rocket* which, apart from being a progenitor of later locomotive development, was an 0-2-2 type with a relatively large driving wheel. Here, at this early stage, we see the polarisation of freight and passenger types; the former needing a smaller driving wheel for starting away with heavy loads, whilst the latter required larger wheels for running with lighter trains at higher speeds. The situation was further clarified later that year when Stephenson introduced his 2-2-0 Planet I type for the Liverpool and Manchester Railway, and shortly afterwards produced his Planet II, which was an 0-4-0 'goods' version of it.

The Planets had Sandwich Frames which were a combination of iron and wood. These provided a backbone and allowed the cylinder to be placed inside. Quite apart from one cylinder block being easier to cast than two separate ones, their location between the frames provided far greater rigidity.

It was now a logical step to the inside-cylinder 0-6-0 which first appeared during the 1830s and was built with innumerable variations over the following century. This was to become the definitive British steam locomotive type as, from the mid nineteenth century virtually until the end of steam traction, it played a major role in freight haulage, especially on those railways which conveyed heavy mineral traffic.

After its inception, the inside-cylinder 0-6-0 quickly established itself on many of the early railways and some classes were built in

George Stephenson's 0-4-0 *Locomotion* seen at the Beamish Open Air Museum. *Locomotion*—an 0-4-0 with cylinders mounted on top of the boiler—made history in 1825 by hauling coal from pits near Darlington to the quayside at Stockton. In fulfilling this duty she was in direct competition with horses. The engine illustrated is a replica of the original specially built for the 150th anniversary of the Stockton & Darlington Railway in 1975. The original *Locomotion* resides at Darlington Railway Museum.

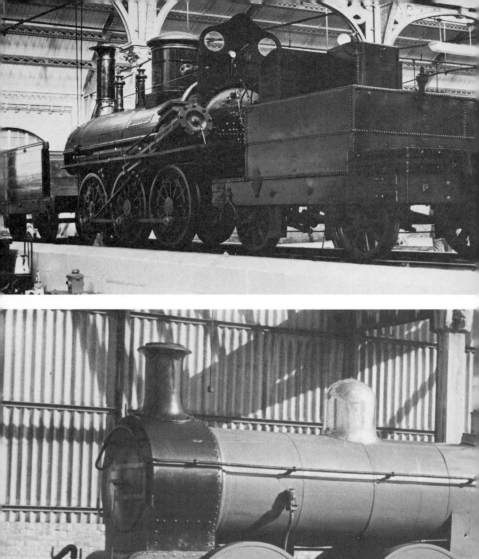

Left

Timothy Hackworth's 0–6–0 *Derwent* of 1845 depicted at Darlington Bank Top Station. Within three years of *Locomotion* being built, the Stockton & Darlington Railway had aspired to six coupled engines and here we see Timothy Hackworth's *Derwent* of 1845. This engine has inclined outside cylinders set at the rear and driving directly onto the first coupled wheels. *Derwent* was one of the few British 0–6–0s with outside cylinders and followed the Stockton & Darlington Railway's principle of using such engines until 1858. *Derwent* was somewhat archaic in having a tender on either side of the engine, the leading one for coal and the rear one for water. Built by W. A. Kitching of Darlington, the engine had 4 ft. diameter driving wheels and 15 in. diameter cylinders and could haul eighty chauldron wagons of coal.

Below

Former South Eastern & Chatham Railway 01 Class 0–6–0, No. 65 designed by Stirling and built at Ashford in 1896 and preserved at the now defunct South Eastern Steam Centre, Ashford. This inside-cylinder 0–6–0 was built during the golden age for this family of engines. She belonged to the South Eastern & Chatham Railway and was one of 122 engines built between 1878 and 1899. In this design—thirty years on from *Derwent*—we find that the cylinders have increased in size to 18 in. diameter and are now firmly established between the frames.

enormous numbers such as Ramsbottom's D Xs of the London & North Western Railway. These splendid engines first appeared in 1858, and almost one thousand were built over the following sixteen years; this was the earliest example in Britain of standardised mass production. During the 1850s another classic genus was commenced by Matthew Kirtley on the Midland Railway and this led to a continuous line of 0-6-0s which culminated in the 4Fs which were perpetuated by the L.M.S. until 1940. The last new design of inside-cylinder 0-6-0s appeared in 1942 with Bulleid's Q1s for the Southern Railway.

With the 0-6-0 firmly established, the next line of development began in 1889 when the first 0-8-0 appeared on the Barry Railway. The 0-8-0 was, in principle, an enlarged 0-6-0 with more power and adhesion. It was destined to see considerable use, almost exclusively in inside-cylinder form. Though powerful, the 0-8-0 was not fast and by the turn of the century the need was felt to speed up certain freight services, not least because many busy networks were becoming cluttered up with slow moving goods trains.

The advent of the 2-8-0 with its leading ponytruck combined the 0-8-0's power with the necessary flexibility for faster running. First introduced by Churchward in 1903 with his 2800 Class, the 2-8-0 was destined to last until the very end of steam. Almost without exception it remained the largest freight type Britain had over the following fifty years, as the policy of frequent trains of modest weight operating on a network characterised by limited siding capacity seldom called for anything larger. Unlike the 0-6-0 and 0-8-0, the 2-8-0 had its cylinders placed outside.

During the early years of the century the 4-6-0 made its appearance in a fast goods guise with such notable designs as Robinson's Fish Engines of 1902 and Fast Goods of 1906. These classes, which were built for the new Great Central Railway, had driving wheel diameters 6 ft. 1 in. and 5 ft. 3 in. respectively. A few other railways adopted similar engines but the 4-6-0 goods hauler truly came into its own from the 1930s as a mixed traffic engine.

Churchward followed his 2800s with a class of mighty 2-8-0Ts for working coal trains from the South Wales valleys to the docks. Though successful, they were an exception in the evolution of freight engines because, apart from shunting and hump work, large tank engines were not employed for main line hauls. The practice of carrying water over

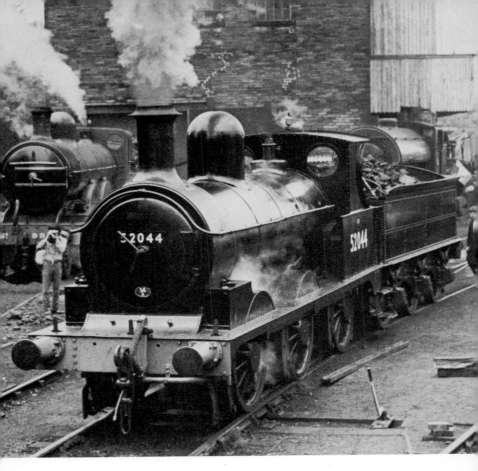

Ex-Lancashire & Yorkshire Railway I/C 0–6–0 designed by Barton Wright and built in 1881. It is seen on the Keighley & Worth Valley Railway. The correlation between the inside-cylinder 0–6–0 goods and the 0–6–0 Saddle Tank was instanced with this design which was built as the standard main line freight engine for the Lancashire & Yorkshire Railway between 1876 and 1887. From 1891 to 1900 many of these 0–6–0s were rebuilt into Saddle Tanks owing to an acute shortage of shunting engines. In this new guise their dimensions and power output remained identical, with 4 ft. 6 in. diameter driving wheels, a cylinder diameter of $17\frac{1}{2}$ in. and a tractive-effort of 17,545 lbs. However, the axle loading on the Saddle Tanks was, of course, greater. Although easily adaptable, relatively few rebuilds of this nature have occurred but this instance does underline the fundamental similarity between the two seemingly different locomotives.

Ex-Great Western Railway, Churchward 2800 Class 2–8–0, No. 2818 built at
Swindon in 1905 and now preserved at the National Railway Museum in York.
The British freight locomotive was destined to change dramatically after 1903
when Churchward introduced Britain's first 2–8–0 with his 2800 Class. This
event was a milestone in locomotive history and heralded the last major phase
in heavy freight power for Britain. The 2–8–0 had bigger cylinders, a higher
boiler pressure and smaller wheels than many of the Victorian period 0–6–0s
and was approximately twice as powerful. The 2800s were well ahead of their
time and magnificent in every way, and building continued in virtually unchanged
form over a thirty-nine year period, the last ones not appearing until 1942.

the driving wheels does provide excellent adhesion for heavy pulling over trackbeds built to a sufficiently high standard.

The second major class of 2-8-0 to appear were Robinson's famous 04s for the Great Central. Introduced in 1911 this type was subsequently taken up by the Railway Operating Division during World War One, and saw widespread use both at home and abroad.

In 1913 Gresley produced his first class of 2-8-0s for the Great Northern to take over from Ivatt's Long Tom 0-8-0s on the coal hauls to London. Five years later Gresley added excitement to the concept with a three-cylinder 2-8-0 but, powerful as these were, the principal reason for their adoption was to enable the engines to start away more easily with heavy loads.

It has already been seen how the 0-6-0 gravitated to the 2-8-0 by means of the 0-8-0 but in 1914 the Midland Railway jumped this evolutionary gap by producing a 2-8-0 as a direct enlargement of their

Great Western Railway 5200 Class 2-8-0T, No. 5239 *Goliath* built at Swindon in 1924. Now preserved on the Torbay and Dartmouth Railway. Having introduced the 2-8-0, Churchward took the freight engine into another area of development when he built this class of heavy 2-8-0Ts in 1910. Intended for short haul coal traffic in the South Wales Valleys, 205 were built over the following thirty years. These were the only 2-8-0Ts ever to run in Britain and though successful some were later rebuilt into 2-8-2Ts and employed on longer main line coal hauls.

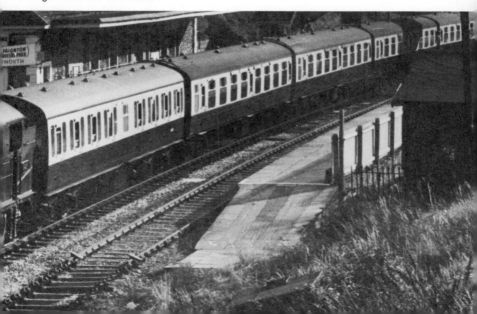

4F 0–6–0. This new design, however, was for the Somerset & Dorset Joint Railway not the Midland who, quite amazingly, continued to ply their heavy coal traffic between Nottinghamshire and London with double-headed 0–6–0s.

It might be imagined that the grouping of Britain's railways in 1923, along with the inevitable rationalisation of motive power, might have produced some dramatic innovations in the size of goods engines as it had in the field of express passenger designs. Although this was not the case, the *pièce de résistance* of British freight engines did appear in 1927 when the L.M.S. adopted Beyer Peacock's idea for a class of 2–6–0 + 0–6–2 Garratts to alleviate the previously mentioned double-heading of 0–6–0s, one Garratt being the equivalent of two engines. Thirty-three of these four-cylinder giants went into operation and, although their evolution was in some respects curious and led nowhere in terms of related development, the Garratts performed well and lasted for almost thirty years.

The multi-cylinder Garratt phase was seen to be nothing more than an interregnum when in 1935 Stanier produced the first of his 8F 2–8–0s. This class eventually totalled almost eight hundred engines and fulfilled the L.M.S. territory's needs until the end of steam. The Great Western continued to build the 2800s whilst on the L.N.E.R. the Robinson and Gresley 2–8–0s adequately fulfilled all requirements. The absence of heavy mineral hauling over the Southern precluded anything larger than an 0–6–0.

World War Two created a demand for more freight engines; initially the Stanier 8F was chosen as a standard type but as the war progressed an Austerity version was prepared by the Ministry of Supply. Over seven hundred engines were built to this pattern. The Americans also chose the 2–8–0 when they built a freight engine for Allied operations; known as the S160, these engines were built to the

Midland Railway Class 4F 0–6–0, No. 43924 built at Derby in 1920. It is seen here on the Keighley and Worth Valley Railway. Despite its vast coalfield traffic the Midland Railway never possessed anything larger than 0–6–0s and, as far as its own operations were concerned, the company seemed oblivious of the exciting developments in 0–8–0 and 2–8–0 traction on other coal carrying railways. Double-heading of Kirtley and Johnson 0–6–0s was rife, but in 1911 the dynasty was upgraded somewhat when Fowler produced his 4F 0–6–0 which represented an increase in power over the Johnson engines. Building continued after the grouping until 1940 when a total of 772 engines had been reached and, at that time, the 4F constituted the most numerous locomotive type in Britain.

British loading gauge and saw considerable service both at home and abroad. Thus, it is interesting to note that the predominant freight power throughout World War Two was almost identical to that employed during World War One—2-8-0s backed up by 0-6-0 and 0-8-0 classes.

However, World War Two did create one precedent which indirectly heralded the final evolutionary strain of British freight engines. That precedent was the introduction of the first 2-10-0. Surprisingly, the intention was to achieve a light axle load rather than greater power and the engines concerned were a ten-coupled version of the Austerity 2-8-0.

Following the nationalisation of Britain's railways in 1948, twelve standard designs were prepared for the entire country and amongst them was a Class 9F 2-10-0. This time the emphasis was not upon a

light axle loading but a heavy mineral engine in its own right with a
tractive-effort of some 40,000 lbs. Thus, the evolution of the British
goods engine had, at the eleventh hour, aspired to ten-coupled
traction—some fifty years after the type had become prevalent in
America and some forty years after its inception in Austria and
Germany. The 0–10–0 phase widely used in Europe was eschewed in
Britain as the light axle load offered was of little benefit whilst its

North Eastern Railway Class Q6 0–8–0, No. 3395 built in 1918 and preserved
on the North Yorkshire Moors Railway. The evolutionary link between the
0–6–0 and 2–8–0 was the 0–8–0, which by the Edwardian period had become
prevalent on several important railways. The 0–8–0 was simply an elongated
0–6–0 and this engine was a member of the North Eastern Railway's two-
cylinder Q6 Class which was introduced in 1913 as part of a progression of
0–8–0s designed between the turn of the century and 1919. The final set, the
Q7s had three cylinders.

Above

Great Western Railway 2251 Class 0-6-0, No. 3205 built at Swindon in 1946 and seen on the Severn Valley Railway. This class of 0-6-0 was introduced by the G.W.R. in 1930 for medium duties and was an updated version of the classic Dean Goods 0-6-0 of 1883 with an almost identical power output. Building continued until nationalisation in 1948 and these engines carried the distinction of being the last inside-cylinder 0-6-0s ever built. Only the advent of the British Railway's standard designs terminated the evolution of the 0-6-0 which from its birth during the 1830s spanned 115 years of building.

Right

Beyer Peacock 0-4-0 + 0-4-0 Garratt built for colliery service in 1937, and now preserved at Bressingham. The Garratt represented the most important variation on the conventional steam locomotive, and one which offered considerable scope for further development had steam traction not become extinct. The first Garratt was built in 1908 by Beyer Peacock of Manchester who adopted the principle and although Garratts featured extensively in exports, only three types ever worked in Britain. These comprised two main line types and one industrial design, and this engine is the sole survivor. She is the last of four 0-4-0 + 0-4-0 Industrial Garratts built between 1924 and 1937 and worked at Baddesley Colliery, Atherstone until withdrawn during the 1960s. Although an industrial, the engine is included in this section as the Garratt was essentially a mainliner and its significance in locomotive evolution lies within this context.

potential power and adhesion for hill climbing was not generally necessary, the greater flexibility of the 2-8-0 (or 2-10-0) being preferred. Similarly, the 2-8-2 and 4-8-0 were not applied; the wide firebox capacity of the former did not have to be exploited because good quality coal was available, whilst the powerful hill climbing capacity of the latter was not needed on Britain's main lines as the smaller mixed traffic designs proved adequate.

The decision to abandon steam traction came within a year of the 9F's appearance and all new development ceased. The new engines soon proved their brilliance for heavy hauling but, by virtue of their 5 ft. diameter driving wheels and finely balanced proportions, they

Above Left
S160 2-8-0, No. 5820 built by Lima in 1945 for the theatre of war in Europe. Now preserved on the Keighley & Worth Valley Railway, it is seen in disguise during the filming of John Sleschinger's *Yanks*. Although not strictly a British engine, the S160 was designed and built in America to supplement the Stanier 8F, and its Austerity variant, during the final years of World War Two. No S160s were taken into British Railways stock following the war, but they did remain widespread in Europe. The S160 represents the excellent combination of a moderately powerful free steaming engine with a light axle load and excellent flexibility, and it formed an essential part in the famous trilogy of 2-8-0s for World War Two.

Below
War Department 2-10-0, No. 600 *Gordon* built by the North British of Glasgow in 1943, and now preserved on the Severn Valley Railway. Britain's first 2-10-0 appeared in 1943 as a light axle load variation on the standard wartime Austerity 2-8-0. This ten-coupled version enabled the axle weights to be reduced from 15 tons 12 cwts to 13 tons 9 cwts. The power output of both types was identical. Twenty-five of 150 built worked in Britain post-war.

showed a remarkable ability to work express passenger trains too, and speeds of 90 mph were recorded—albeit, such practices were eventually forbidden by the operating authorities.

And so, the trusty British 0–6–0 drudge had finally turned into a highly sophisticated engine, for the 9F represented the perfect climax to British freight locomotive development. When considering the major role the inside-cylinder 0–6–0 played over one and one quarter centuries it is amazing that its absolute displacement came within an incredibly narrow space of time, the Southern Railway's Q1 appearing only eleven years before the first 9F.

The last steam locomotive built for British Railways was a 9F and this engine, completed in 1960 as the last in a class of 250 engines, took the name *Evening Star*. Whatever the restricted confines within the epoch of the British freight locomotive, the two outer limits of *Locomotion* and *Evening Star* represent a thrilling evolutionary contrast.

British Railways Class 9F, 2–10–0 No. 92203 *Black Prince*, built in 1959 and now preserved on the East Somerset Railway. The ultimate British freight engines were the 9F 2–10–0s which provided a considerable advance in versatility and power over the 2–8–0. Sadly, the 9F had a short working life and, owing to the abandonment of steam traction, some were broken up only a few years after being built—a marked contrast with some of their ancestors, the near centenarian 0–6–0s!

SECTION 3

Express Passenger Locomotives

The story of how Stephenson's *Rocket* won the Rainhill Trials in 1829 and its subsequent adoption for use on the first passenger carrying railway between Liverpool and Manchester is widely known. But, apart from laying down some of the fundamental concepts on which later locomotives were based, *Rocket* was the first passenger engine. She was an o-2-2 with a large driving wheel for stability at speed, and it is claimed that she travelled at the unprecedented speed of 39 mph.

Within a few years of *Rocket*'s inception, two distinct strains of passenger locomotive evolved; the first was pioneered by *Rocket* which had the firebox placed behind the driving wheels, whilst the second, which began with the 2-4-0, had its firebox set between the coupled axles. The first of these strains culminated in the Pacific, which represented the zenith of express steam in Britain, and the second ended with the 4-6-0 which became the premier type until superseded by the Pacific from the mid-1930s.

In following the strain commenced by *Rocket* we find that the o-2-2 was not sufficiently stable once speeds increased, and a logical progression was the 2-2-2, notable amongst which were the Jenny Linds; these were built for several early railways by E. B. Wilson's works in Leeds. This line of development supported a bigger boiler and firebox, as did the emergent 2-2-0s and o-4-2s.

As the century progressed, the small single wheelers, which were by far the most predominant type, showed limitations in the continuing quest for heavier and faster trains. This led to the adoption of the 4-2-2 which had first been introduced by Gooch for the Great Western Railway in 1847. Although the 2-2-2 remained in service well into the nineteenth century, the larger 4-2-2 with its superior flexibility became the most advanced type of Single. It saw use on many railways and although increasingly heavier trains posed diffi-culties owing to the lack of adhesion, the advent of steam sanding apparatus helped alleviate the problem, and the last examples appeared as late as 1901. The 4-2-2 was extremely fleet-footed and speeds of

Left
L.N.W.R. Precedent Class 2-4-0, No. 790 *Hardwicke* built at Crewe in 1892 and now preserved at the National Railway Museum in York. The 2-4-0 was the principal form of express passenger engine until the 1880s, and appeared in many forms. For trains up to 250 tons it proved fast and economical. The L. & N.W.R. used the type prolifically over the West Coast main line until well into the present century, and one of the stalwarts was the Precedent Class introduced in 1874. These diminutive engines were thrashed unmercifully over the L. & N.W.R's main lines as was evidenced by the constant patter of cinders falling on the coach roofs. It was not until 1904 that the Precedents were extended to create the celebrated Precursor 4-4-0s.

Above
Great Northern Railway Ivatt 'Small Atlantic' 4-4-2, No. 990 *Henry Oakley* built at Doncaster in 1898, and preserved at the National Railway Museum in York. The Atlantic era was heralded in 1898 when Ivatt introduced this class of 4-4-2 for the Great Northern. These original engines had their fireboxes contained within the frames, but the larger version which appeared in 1902 had the extra wide grate which fanned out over the trailing wheels in true Atlantic fashion. At the time of their inception, these 'Large Atlantics' were the biggest passenger engines in Britain.

90 mph were achieved. As a family of engines, the Singles remained active for one century from their inception in 1829, until their final displacement from main line duties during the 1920s.

A fascinating evolutionary quirk occurred in 1882, when Stroudley introduced his 0-4-2 Gladstones. The 0-4-2 had first appeared as a passenger engine in 1838 with *Lion* on the Liverpool and Manchester Railway, but the type had never been seriously considered for fast running, as the absence of leading wheels was potentially hazardous. However, Stroudley—who did not care for bogies—claimed that fast running could be achieved with the driving wheels in the lead, and in the event was proved correct, the Gladstones being excellent runners.

The Single's generic characteristics took a new turn when the first Atlantic 4-4-2 appeared on the Great Northern Railway in 1898. Hitherto, the G.N. had used 2-2-2s and 4-2-2s. These Atlantics were an enlargement of the 4-2-2s and, in common with the Single family, had their firebox set behind the rear driving axle. This enabled the grate to spread outwards without obstruction from the coupled axles, and permitted the use of a more powerful engine to cope with the ever increasing demands for faster and heavier main line expresses. So began the Atlantic Era, which embraced many railways from the turn

Above Left
Midland Railway Johnson three-cylinder Compound 4–4–0, No. 1000 built at
Derby in 1902, and now preserved at The National Railway Museum in York.
Commensurate with the G.N. Atlantics came the first three-cylinder 4–4–0s
on the North Eastern Railway. Apart from advancing the power of the
established inside-cylinder variety, these new engines were Compounds in
which the steam from one large high-pressure cylinder was exhausted into
two low-pressure ones outside. This inception led to the celebrated Midland
Compounds which first appeared in 1902 and, apart from becoming the
principal main line power for the Midland Railway for the remainder of its
existence, played an important part in working express trains on the L.M.S.
under whom building continued. These Midland engines are regarded as the
most successful compound type ever built in Britain. They remained as an
important passenger type for some years after the grouping, and achieved
distinction in working the London–Birmingham two-hour expresses.

Above
Great Northern Railway Gresley Pacific 4–6–2, No. 4472 *Flying Scotsman* built
at Doncaster in 1923 and now preserved at Steamtown in Carnforth.
Locomotive history was made in 1922 when Gresley introduced his first
three-cylinder Pacific for the Great Northern. Building of these engines
continued until 1935, albeit with various modifications including a higher
boiler pressure of 220 lbs per sq. in. They were appropriately named after
famous racehorses, and without any doubt were one of the finest express
passenger designs of all time, both in terms of performance and appearance.
Named after the celebrated London–Edinburgh express which she often
worked, *Flying Scotsman* is probably the world's most famous steam locomotive.

of the century until well after World War One.

The Atlantic Era was one of flamboyance and led directly to the Pacific which, in essence, was a big Atlantic with an extra pair of driving wheels. When Gresley introduced his A1 Pacifics onto the Great Northern in 1922, they represented, in terms of size and power, as large an increase over the G.N.'s biggest Atlantics as the first Atlantics of 1898 exerted over the earlier 4-2-2 Singles. Such progress over a mere twenty-three years contrasts greatly with developments in goods engines, and demonstrates the tremendous pressures to which the express passenger locomotive was subjected throughout its entire evolution. Nevertheless, the Pacific represented the end of the evolutionary line, and although more powerful examples were to come, nothing bigger ever appeared for Britain, apart from Gresley's thrilling but brief incursions into huge 2-8-2 Mikados and his solitary 4-6-4.

From the outset, the British Pacific was conceived as a multi-cylinder machine. Here again the influence of Churchward must be acknowledged, not just for producing Britain's first Pacific, *The Great Boar*, in 1908, but for synthesising in it the best of contemporary continental multi-cylinder practise as represented by the de Glelm/du Bousquet Atlantics of 1904. Even though *The Great Boar* remained a solo experiment that was not repeated on the G.W.R., its lessons were absorbed by both Stanier and Gresley, and through Gresley, Bulleid, and perpetuated for the next forty years.

The super-power prestige of the Pacifics captured the popular imagination both during the heyday of the high speed steam train and since, for today Britain's most famous preserved engines are of the Pacific type. As a family of locomotives, the British Pacific falls into four principal genera: the three-cylinder G.N./L.N.E.R. group based upon Doncaster, embracing the designs of Gresley, Thompson and Peppercorn; the four-cylinder L.M.S. group centred upon Crewe

Great Western Railway Castle Class 4-6-0, No. 5051 *Drysllwyn Castle* built at Swindon in 1936, and now preserved by the Great Western Society at Didcot. Commensurate with Gresley producing his three-cylinder Pacific for the Great Northern, Collet introduced his four-cylinder Castle 4-6-0 for the G.W.R. These engines were, in accordance with G.W. practice, a continuation of the magnificent locomotive tradition laid down by Churchward during the Edwardian period, and constituted an enlarged version of his four-cylinder Star 4-6-0s. The Castles proved to be brilliant engines, and they exerted considerable influence on locomotive development—not least on the under-powered L.M.S. The class totalled 171 engines, and building continued until 1950.

Great Western Railway King Class 4–6–0, No. 6000 *King George V*. Built at Swindon in 1927, this magnificent engine is preserved at Bulmers in Hereford. The 4–6–0 remained supreme on the Great Western. The gravitation to Pacific power was never made, as all top duties were ably handled by the four-cylinder Kings of 1927. In addition to having an identical tractive-effort to the L.M.S. Pacifics, the Kings were also considerably lighter, and tipped the scales in full working order at 136 tons, compared with the 160 ton weight of a Princess Royal.

with the designs of Stanier; the three–cylinder S.R. group designed by Bulleid from Eastleigh, and, finally, the two and three–cylinder types built under the nationalised British Railways at Crewe from 1951 onwards.

The success of the A1s led Gresley to produce his streamlined A4 in 1935. Competition for Scottish traffic was keen between the East and West Coast routes during the early 1930s, and the new engines enabled a considerable speeding up of services. The 1930s were a time when streamlining was fashionable and generated much publicity. The A4s proved to be the 'Concordes' of their day and have become the most celebrated British locomotive type—not least since No. 4468 *Mallard* achieved the world speed record for steam of 126 mph in 1938. It is fascinating to think that in less than forty years, express passenger locomotive evolution on the East Coast Route evolved from graceful Victorian styled 4–2–2 Singles to the 'supersonic' modernity of the streamlined A4s.

Events on the West Coast main line took a dramatic turn in 1933 when Stanier, who had received his training at Swindon under

L.N.E.R. Class D49 4–4–0, No. 246 *Morayshire* built in 1928 and preserved by
the Scottish Railway Preservation Society at Falkirk. The year 1927, noted for
the G.W. King Class, and the L.M.S. Royal Scot Class, also saw the introduction
of the L.N.E.R. D49 4–4–0 which Gresley built with three-cylinders in
continuance of his general policy. These interesting engines were similar in
power to the first Great Northern Atlantics, and their boiler was identical
to that fitted onto Gresley's J39 Class of inside-cylinder 0–6–0 goods of the
previous year. Intended for secondary express passenger work, the Shires
and Hunts, as the class became known, proved rugged performers and they
paved the way for the Southern Railway's Schools Class in 1930, and the very
last of the lineage, the Great Northern Railway of Ireland's three-cylinder
4–4–0s of 1948.

Churchward, introduced his Princess Royal Pacifics. In anticipation
of faster services between London and Scotland, No. 6201 *Princess
Elizabeth* made an epic non-stop test run over the 401 miles from
Glasgow–Euston in 5¾ hours. In 1937 Stanier designed an improved
version of the Princess Royals called the Coronations, which, in
common with the A4s, were streamlined.

The Southern Railway's first Pacifics did not appear until 1941,
when Oliver Bulleid, who had been Gresley's assistant at Doncaster,
introduced his air-smoothed Merchant Navy Class. These engines
included many new features and were followed in 1945 by a lighter
and less powerful version, known as the West Countries and Battle of
Britains.

During the late 1950s many of Bulleid's Pacifics were rebuilt to a
more conventional form, and as a result remained on main line
expresses until 1967. During their last few years, they brought the

Above
L.M.S. Stanier Princess Royal Pacific 4–6–2, No. 6201 *Princess Elizabeth* built
at Crewe in 1933 and preserved at Bulmers in Hereford. Stanier tackled the
L.M.S.'s need for a truly powerful engine on its West Coast Main Line in 1933
with his Princess Royal Pacifics. Stanier had left the Great Western to take up
the post of Chief Mechanical Engineer of the L.M.S. and the Princess Royals
were in many respects a Pacific version of the G.W.'s King Class.

Right
L.N.E.R. Streamlined A 4 Pacific, No. 60009 *Union of South Africa* built at
Doncaster in 1937 and preserved on the Lochty Railway in Fife. The most
celebrated British locomotive class is the Gresley A4, first introduced for the
crack expresses of the L.N.E.R.'s East Coast Main Line in 1935. These streamlined descendants of Gresley's earlier A1s proved incredibly fast, and during
speed trials one ran at 100 mph for forty-three continuous miles and averaged
91 mph for seventy miles. Furthermore, during *Mallard*'s record breaking dash
in 1938, 120 mph was averaged for five miles.

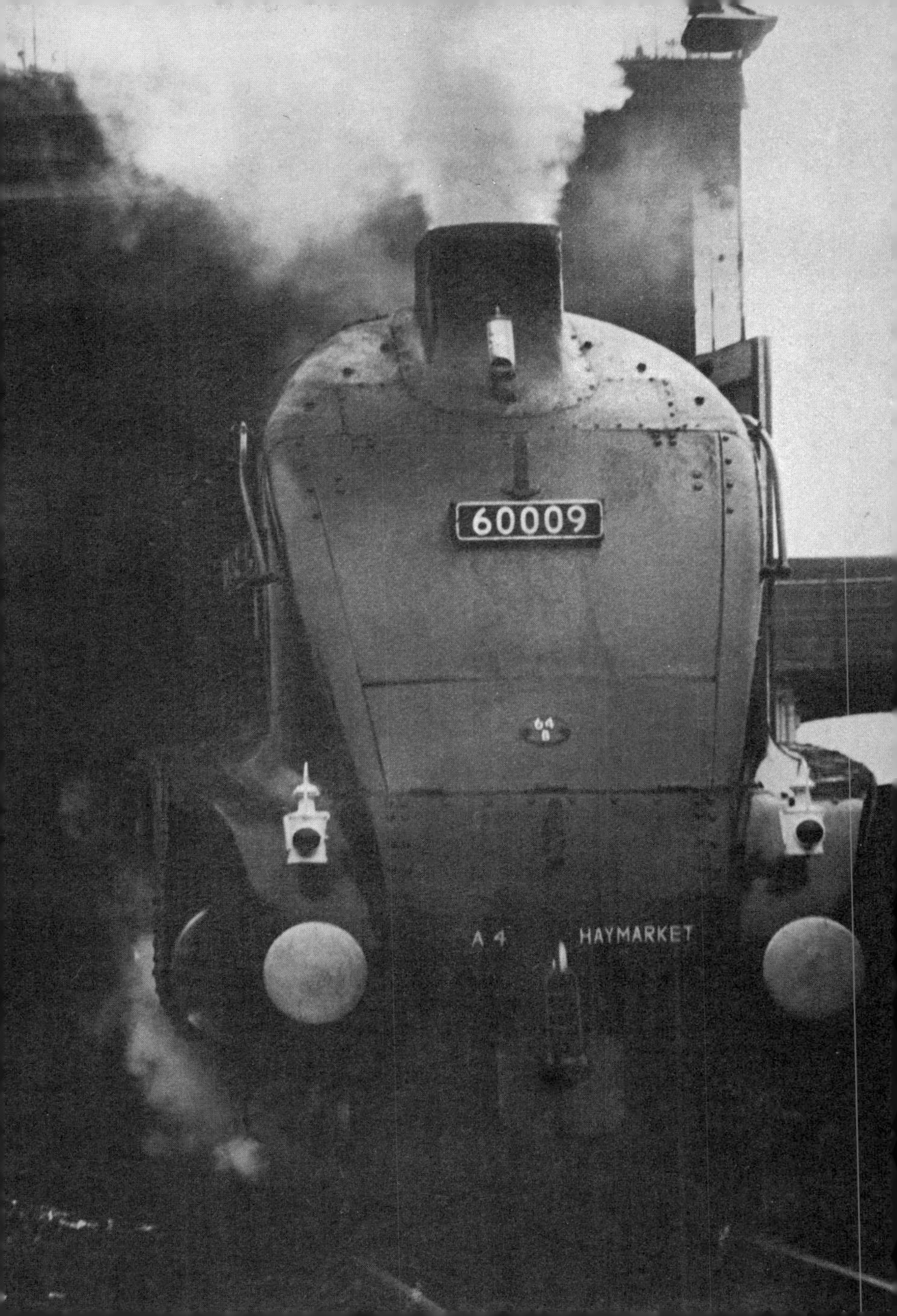
60009
A 4
HAYMARKET

British Pacific locomotive tradition to a fitting conclusion with some spirited 100 mph dashes over the racing ground between London (Waterloo) and Bournemouth.

The Pacific was chosen as the principal express passenger type under the standardisation programme of British Railways, and in 1951 the Festival of Britain proudly displayed the first example, No. 70000 *Britannia*, much as the Wembley Exhibition had displayed Gresley's A1 in 1924. The Britannias, along with the smaller Clans, were the only two-cylinder Pacifics to run in Britain, and were intended for all but the heaviest of main line duties.

A larger three-cylinder version of the Britannias appeared in 1954. Named *Duke of Gloucester*, this engine was intended to be the forerunner of a new heavy express passenger class, but the decision to dispense with steam traction prevented any further examples from being built, and it was with this historic engine that evolution had its final fling—exactly 125 years after the building of *Rocket*!

As indicated at the beginning of this section, the other strain of express passenger engine began with the 2-4-0 during the 1830s and this wheel arrangement became prevalent as the nineteenth century progressed. The 2-4-0 was widely used on many railways as it possessed a better starting and pulling ability than the Single. The most prodigious feat of 2-4-0 performance on record concerns the running made by the L. & N.W.R. Jumbo, No. 790 *Hardwicke* when, as part of the railway races in 1895, she covered the 141 miles from Crewe-Carlisle at an average speed of 67.2 mph!

As the large Single gravitated to the Atlantic, a similar metamorphosis occurred with the 2-4-0, when in response to traffic demands, it progressed naturally into an inside-cylinder 4-4-0. The first appeared during the 1870s and so was born one of the most graceful locomotive types of all time. The late nineteenth century was a period of extremely skilful designing, and the naturally balanced proportions of the 4-4-0, combined with a driving wheel diameter of up to 7 ft., led to some extremely shapely and beautiful locomotives, the examples built by Johnson for the Midland Railway in 1876 being but one

No. 21C 123 *Blackmore Vale,* a Southern Railway unrebuilt West Country Pacific 4-6-2, which is preserved on the Bluebell Railway. A slightly smaller version of the Bulleid's Merchant Navy Class 4-6-2s, the West Country and Battle of Britain Class were termed Light Pacifics and were permitted to work almost anywhere on the southern system by reason of their lighter axle loading.

instance. In common with the 2-4-0, the firebox remained between the coupled axles, but the leading bogie provided extra stability for negotiating curves at speed. The inside-cylinder 4-4-0 became the principal express passenger type of the late Victorian and Edwardian periods.

An example of express passenger power active towards the close of the nineteenth century, can be given by studying the engines used in the Great Railway Races between London and Aberdeen in 1895:

West Coast Route
London & North Western Railway

London (Euston)–Crewe	Three-cylinder Compound Teutonic 2-4-0
Crewe–Carlisle	Two-cylinder Precedent 2-4-0 *Hardwicke*
Caledonian Railway	
Carlisle–Aberdeen	Inside-cylinder 4-4-0, 6 ft. 6 in. diameter wheels

East Coast Route
Great Northern Railway

London (Kings Cross)–York	Stirling 8 ft. Single 4-2-2
North Eastern Railway	
York–Edinburgh	Inside-cylinder 4-4-0, M Class
North British Railway	
Edinburgh–Aberdeen	Inside-cylinder 4-4-0, 6 ft. 6 in. diameter wheels.

The brilliance of their performances can be appreciated by the West Coast Route's time of 512 minutes for the 540 miles from London to Aberdeen in 8½ hours in 1895!

The 1890s were a watershed period in passenger locomotive development. Considerable improvements to the permanent way had been made by this time, whilst the increasing use of restaurant and sleeping car services inevitably meant heavier trains. Only one year after the Single gravitated into an Atlantic in 1898, an equally significant progression advanced the 4-4-0 into the 4-6-0 with ten engines built for the North Eastern Railway. Within three years 4-6-0s were active on the Highland, Great Western, Caledonian and Great Central.

By the 1923 grouping, the 4-6-0—in both two and four-cylinder form—was widespread and, having usurped the Atlantic, had firmly assumed the role as the principal heavy express passenger type for Britain.

A new phase of development in express passenger locomotives occurred in 1907, when the London, Brighton & South Coast Railway built a class of superheated 4-4-2 tank engines for work between London and the South Coast. These amazing engines were followed in 1908 when the Lancashire and Yorkshire, having introduced their four-cylinder 4-6-0s, simultaneously produced a 4-6-4 tank version. Soon afterwards the L.B.S.C.R. built a pair of 4-6-2s and a class of 4-6-4Ts and employed them on the London (Victoria)-Brighton expresses, on which they remained until ousted by electrification in 1932. The big express passenger tanks were a fascinating family of engines but, apart from obvious limitations in fuel capacity, claims of unsteadiness at speed were often made, and they contributed little to the overall pattern of evolution, and as a concept had fizzled out prior to the grouping.

Despite the Pacific's advent in 1922, the claim to be the most powerful express passenger locomotive remained with the four-cylinder 4-6-0 throughout the 1920s, firstly with the G.W. Castles of 1923, then the S.R.'s Lord Nelsons in 1926, and finally with the ultimate in British 4-6-0s, the G.W. Kings of 1927. The first Stanier Pacific in 1933 ostensibly took the title from the Kings, although the Princesses had an identical tractive-effort. From this it can be seen that the G.W., in burning superior Welsh coal, never needed to develop the Pacific—the firegrate area of the King being a mere 34 sq. ft. as compared with 45 sq. ft. on the Princess Royals.

In 1930 the 4-4-0 made its last brilliant flourish with the Southern Railway's three-cylinder Schools, the most powerful engines of this wheel arrangement ever to run in Britain. From the mid-1930s, the 4-6-0 became increasingly used as the basis for powerful two-cylinder mixed traffic types. In this guise, it continued to play an important role on main line passenger duties. With Britain's policy of frequent and relatively light trains, the 4-6-0, despite its restricted firebox capacity, was sufficient, with the quality of the coal available, to provide the necessary power and adhesion for most express duties until the end of steam, and the next logical step to the 4-8-0, although proposed, was never actually taken.

SECTION 4

Narrow Gauge Locomotives

Britain's railways were built in a piecemeal way under private enterprise and, bearing this in mind, it is remarkable that the nation's gauge was developed so consistently to a standard 4 ft. 8½ in. Gauges smaller than standard were constructed in a way that augmented the national system rather than conflicted with it. British narrow gauge railways fell into three principal categories: first came the lines allied to certain industries or manufacturing complexes; secondly, rural lines for conveying general goods and passengers; and thirdly, miniature lines with a gauge of only 15 in. In general, the locomotives were individualistically styled, their design being derived from the immediate needs of the line, but, in many cases, especially on the industrial networks and miniature systems, they were essentially scaled down versions of standard gauge designs.

The first steam worked narrow gauge railway in the world was the Festiniog. Built to a gauge of 1 ft. 11½ in. in 1836, the line originally used horses to convey slate over the 12¾ mile long route from Blaenau Festiniog to Portmadoc Harbour. Steam locomotives took over in 1863 and were an immediate success despite initial doubts from none other than Robert Stephenson, as to the practicability of using engines on so narrow a gauge. Apart from being the forerunner of narrow gauge engines the world over, the early Festiniog examples were 0-4-0 tender-tanks. This was a rare concept in British locomotive development as tender and tank engines almost always evolved independently, and any such pairings were usually an act of hybridisation on the part of their owners.

Following an increased demand for slate, the Festiniog achieved world fame in 1869 by adopting the powerful double-ended Fairlie; this was a locomotive invertebrate and an early ancestor of the Mallet, Kitson Meyer and Garratt articulateds. The Fairlie's strangeness was matched on other Welsh slate lines by the equally remarkable De Winton, an 0-4-0 tank with a vertical boiler which enabled hills to be climbed without the elements becoming uncovered. The De Wintons

Festiniog Railway 0-4-4-0T, Fairlie *Merddia Emerys* built in 1879 at the
Festiniog Railway's Boston Lodge Works. This early form of articulated
locomotive, known as the Fairlie, first appeared in 1865. Most Fairlies consisted
of a double boiler engine with a common central firebox. The twin boiler
was mounted on two power bogies which enabled these powerful engines to
negotiate tight curves, and to have all their axles available for adhesion. The
Fairlie achieved considerable recognition, but had the disadvantage of a
limited fuel capacity and high maintenance costs, which led to its demise in
favour of other articulateds. The Festiniog Railway was the only serious user
of the type in Britain, and in 1979 the company constructed a new Fairlie
which incorporated parts of an 1885 built engine.

De Winton 0–4–0VBT, *Chaloner* built by De Winton of Caernarvon in 1877
and preserved on the Leighton Buzzard Narrow Gauge Railway. The De
Winton was a strange vertical boilered engine built for the slate industry of
North Wales. The two cylinders were bolted on to the boiler, and the drive
was direct by means of a crank axle. The De Winton was the principal
standard type for the railways of the Welsh slate quarries before the advent
of the Quarry Hunslets.

had vertical valve gear; accordingly no springs could be fitted and the engines, though robust, were extremely rough to work on. These amazing machines were built exclusively for the Welsh slate industry by De Winton & Co., of Caernarvon, and they took over from horses in many quarries. Building was undertaken to both 2 ft. and 3 ft. gauge, and at least sixty examples were put to work between 1869 and the end of the century.

Neither the Fairlie or the De Winton had any influence upon subsequent British locomotive development, and whilst the former did spread to other parts of the world, the De Winton evolved, flowered and died amid the slate mountains of North Wales.

The Welsh slate industry was a breeding ground for narrow gauge railways and in 1866 the Tallylyn opened with 0-4-0 and 0-4-2 tanks. Amid the diversity of motive power which occurred as the various quarries adopted locomotives, two standard conventional types emerged—the Quarry Hunslet and the Main Line Hunslet. These engines were, in effect, scaled down Leeds contractor's type 0-4-0 Saddle Tanks; the smaller quarry variety was used on the various ledges from which the slate was taken, whilst the main line engines conveyed the loaded trains to the quaysides.

The first cross country system to adopt narrow gauge was the Isle of Man Railway, which opened in 1873. A gauge of 3 ft. was chosen and Beyer Peacock supplied a class of 2-4-0Ts which were a smaller version of their standard gauge 4-4-0Ts supplied in 1864 to the Metropolitan Railway for use on the first suburban workings in London. This is a perfect case of cross-fertilisation; not just of gauge, but also between suburban and cross country types. Other 3 ft. gauge lines, such as the famous Southwold in Suffolk, also adopted scaled down designs, as witness their Sharp Stewart 2-4-0Ts for passenger work and Manning Wardle 0-6-2T for goods traffic.

The soaring demand for North Wales slate during the nineteenth century was matched by the need for iron ore, and extensive development occurred over the Northamptonshire Ironstone Bed which extends from central Lincolnshire to Oxfordshire. The main activities centred upon Northamptonshire, and although many lines were built to standard gauge—such as the vast network centred upon Corby— some narrow gauge systems appeared. One of the best known was centred upon Kettering Ironworks which operated Manning Wardle 0-6-0STs and Black Hawthorn 0-4-0STs. Once again, these were primarily scaled down versions of the manufacturers standard gauge designs for industry.

An entirely new concept in British narrow gauge locomotive evolution occurred in North Wales when the Snowdon Mountain Railway was opened in 1895 to carry tourists from Llanberis to the summit of Snowdon. The gradients were as steep as 1 in $5\frac{1}{2}$, and prohibited the use of conventional traction. Accordingly special 0-4-2Ts, incorporating the Abt Rack and Pinion System, were imported from the Swiss Locomotive Works who had achieved considerable expertise in building such engines. However, it is interesting to note that the first application of the rack and pinion

Beyer Peacock 2-4-0T, No. 5 *Mona*, built for the Isle of Man Railway in 1874, and preserved on the Isle of Man Victorian Steam Railway. She is seen heading a train near St. John's. The 3 ft. gauge Isle of Man Railway opened in 1873, the first cross-country narrow gauge railway. Beyer Peacock built a large family of similar engines for various gauges.

principle was at the Middleton Colliery, Leeds, in 1812—albeit because the designer thought that a conventional engine would not grip the rails if pulling a load!

The building of narrow gauge railways was given a boost in 1896, when the Light Railway Act was passed. This legislation permitted secondary lines to be built to lower standards than the statutory ones. The act stated that providing trains were run at restricted speeds, a lighter track and simplified signalling system would be permissible. This arrangement also allowed industrial lines to carry passengers. The Light Railway Order granted to our preserved railways today operates under a similar principle.

Two railways immediately followed this act, the 1 ft. $11\frac{1}{2}$ in. gauge Vale of Rheidol and the 2 ft. 6 in. gauge Welshpool and Llanfair, which became known as the Farmers' Line. The former employed 2-6-2Ts rather surprisingly built by the celebrated locomotive injector company of Davies and Metcalfe of Romily, although the engines were in effect an enlargement of a design which Manning Wardle built for the Lynton and Barnstaple Railway in North Devon. In contrast, motive power on the W. & L. consisted of Beyer Peacock 0-6-0Ts.

Shortly after the turn of the century a fascinating industrial line developed in Kent when Edward Lloyd opened a 2 ft. 6 in. gauge system at his Sittingbourne Paper Mills. Initially, three Kerr Stuart 0-4-2STs took over from horses, but as the network expanded larger 0-6-2Ts were added. This was one of Britain's most interesting industrial railways, and it is fortunate that a section of it remains active under preservation.

A new family of narrow gauge engines was created during World War One. These engines were vitally employed at establishments throughout Britain, transporting military stores and armaments, whilst in Europe they plied from standard gauge railheads to the trenches. Initially, Hunslet built one hundred 4-6-0Ts for this work but more were urgently needed, and Baldwins of Philadelphia supplied their own 4-6-0T design, and built no less than 495 examples between March 1916 and April 1917. They were rugged engines but rather ungainly by virtue of a high centre of gravity, and a 2-6-2T variation was subsequently supplied by the American Locomotive Company (Alco). After extensive military service, examples of the three types found their way on to various narrow gauge lines in both Britain and Europe, although many were sent to India for working on the newly

Above

Quarry Hunslet type 0–4–0ST, No. 3 *Dolbadarn* built by Hunslet in 1922 and preserved on the Llanberis Lake Railway. This engine represents a miniature version of Hunslet's standard gauge contractors type 0–4–0ST. First introduced in 1882 for the slate industry of North Wales, this 2 ft. gauge type was known as the 'Quarry Hunslet' and was a more powerful engine than the De Winton. This successful miniaturisation of a standard gauge design remained at work until 1968, and outlived the famous Kerr Stuart 'Wren' class and E type Barclay, built for similar duties.

Right

A Main Line Hunslet 0–4–0ST of 2 ft. gauge built in 1893. Named *Linda,* this engine is depicted in rebuilt form as a 2–4–0STT. She is preserved on the Festiniog Railway. It was conceived as a larger version of the type previously illustrated. Under preservation she has been rebuilt as a tender engine for longer range running on the Festiniog Railway. This rebuild demonstrates the adaptability of the basic Leeds design for duties never imagined ninety years ago.

developed sugar plantations. Recently the Festiniog Railway acquired one of the Alco 2-6-2Ts from France and under the name of *Mountaineer* she works today as testimony to this historic family of locomotives built specifically for wartime operations.

Another system under active preservation is the 2 ft. gauge Leighton Buzzard Railway which was built to carry sand up to the London and North Western main line. Steam was only used briefly around 1920

Vale of Rheidol Railway 2–6–2T, No. 9 *Prince of Wales* built by Davies and Metcalfe in 1902 and run today by British Rail with the aid of a supporting society. Similarities in locomotive design often occur as a result of one manufacturer taking the design of another and building similar engines, albeit with detail variations. This engine represents a perfect example having been built by Davies and Metcalfe in 1902, based around a 2–6–2T design which Manning Wardle prepared in 1897. The 2–6–2T was at this time an advanced concept for the narrow gauge, and had not appeared on any main line.

before petrol and diesel powered Simplex engines were adopted. However, since a large part of the railway has been acquired for preservation, the line has become a veritable repository of varied narrow gauge locomotives including a British 'Colonial Export' returned home from overseas.

In Ireland, the 3 ft. gauge became an accepted standard for many secondary lines. Motive power consisted almost entirely of tank engines with a preponderance of four-coupled types. However, all British Conventions were broken in 1905 when the Londonderry and Lough Swilly Railway introduced two 4-8-0s from Hudswell Clark. These were followed in 1912 by a 4-8-4 tank version. No other British railway ever ran 4-8-0s or 4-8-4Ts.

At the opposite end of the scale from operations in Ireland, came the dimunitive engines which operated over the 18 in. gauge networks inside the locomotive works at Horwich and Crewe. These systems were devised for carrying stores throughout the plant, where confines were inevitably restricted. Horwich built eight 0-4-0STs for this duty between 1887 and 1901, and the last survivor was not withdrawn until 1962. Appropriately named *Wren*, this engine now resides in the National Railway Museum. The Crewe system succumbed during the early 1930s but two of the engines, named *Pet* and *Dot*, can be seen in the Narrow Gauge Museum of the Tallylyn Railway at Towyn.

Lines built to gauges smaller than 18 in. are usually referred to as miniature, and three famous railways have been built within this category: The Ravenglass and Eskdale, The Romney Hythe and Dymchurch, and The Fairbourne. All have a gauge of 15 in. and all survive in preserved form. Motive power invariably consists of scaled down main line designs, but within the 15 in. gauge, three distinct patterns of evolution can be traced: the Basset Lowke, the Greenly and the Heywood.

Basset Lowke built engines as true $\frac{1}{4}$ scale versions of the original, the Fairbourne Railway's Atlantic *Count Louis* being an example. Under the Greenly tradition, engines were built to $\frac{1}{3}$ scale for additional power, and the locomotives of the Romney Hythe and Dymchurch are examples of this practice. Finally, under the Heywood tradition, engines were built as large as was reasonably possible following a principle which has its roots in the 15 in. gauge Duffield Bank Railway of Sir Arthur Heywood; *Northern Rock* on the Ravenglass and Eskdale personifies this approach.

1 Canterbury & Whitstable Railway 0-4-0, *Invicta* built by Robert Stephenson in 1830 and preserved at Poor Priests Hospital in Canterbury.

2 Kitson 0–6–2T, No. 29 built in 1904 and preserved on the North Yorkshire Moors Railway.

3 North Eastern Railway Class J27 0–6–0, No. 2392 built in 1923. This engine currently resides at the National Railway Museum in York.

4 Lancashire and Yorkshire Railway 0–4–0ST Pug, No. 51218 built in 1901 and preserved on the Keighley and Worth Valley Railway.

5 L.M.S. Stanier Jubilee 4–6–0, No. 5690 *Leander* built in 1936 and preserved at Steamtown in Carnforth.

6 Norwegian State Railway Mogul 2–6–0, No. 19 built by Nohab in 1919 and preserved on the Kent and East Sussex Railway.

7 Southern Railway rebuilt West Country Pacific, No. 34016 *Bodmin* built in 1948, and preserved at Bulmers in Hereford.

8 G.W.R. Manor Class 4–6–0, No. 7827 *Lydham Manor* built in 1950 and preserved on the Torbay and Dartmouth Railway.

9 Borrows 0–4–0 Well Tank type, *Windle* built in 1909 and seen on the Middleton Railway.

10 Avonside 1 ft. 11½ in. gauge 0–4–0T, No. 4 *Sezela* built in 1916 and preserved at Knebworth West Park and Winter Green Railway.

11 R.S.H. 56 Class 0–6–0ST, No. 26 built in 1950 and seen on the Kent & East Sussex Railway.

12 Midland Railway Johnson 'Spinner' 4-2-2, No. 673 built at Derby in 1890 and now preserved at the National Railway Museum in York.

13 Caledonian Railway Single 4-2-2, No. 123 built by Neilsons of Glasgow in 1886 and now preserved in the Glasgow Transport Museum.

14 London & South Western Railway Drummond Class T9 4–4–0, No. 120 built in 1899 and now preserved at The National Railway Museum in York.

15 Midland Railway Kirtley 2–4–0, No. 158A built at Derby in 1866 and preserved at the Midland Railway Centre, Butterley.

16 Great Eastern Railway J15 Class 0-6-0, No. 564 built in 1912 and preserved on the North Norfolk Railway.

17 L.N.E.R. Class K1 2–6–0, No. 2005 built in 1949 and preserved on the North Yorkshire Moors Railway.

18 London & South Western Railway Adams 4–4–2T, No. 488 built in 1885 by Neilson of Glasgow and preserved on the Bluebell Railway.

19 Southern Railway unrebuilt West Country Pacific 4–6–2, No. 21C 123 *Blackmore Vale* built in 1946 and preserved on the Bluebell Railway.

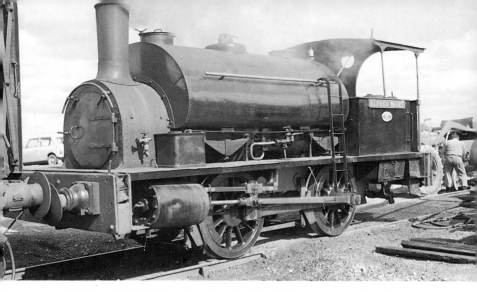

20 Neilson 0–4–0ST Pug, *Alfred Paget* built in 1882 and preserved on the
Chasewater Light Railway.

21 Manning Wardle type 0–6–0ST built by Robert Stephenson & Hawthorn
as works number 7031 in 1941. This engine is seen on the Stour Valley Railway.

22 L.M.S. Stanier 8F 2–8–0, No. 8233 built by the North British Locomotive Company, Glasgow in 1940. She is depicted on the Severn Valley Railway.

23 Great Northern Railway 0–6–0ST, No. 1247 built in 1899 at Doncaster and preserved at the National Railway Museum, York.

24 Great Western Railway 1361 Class 0–6–0ST, No. 1363 built in 1910 and preserved by the Great Western Society at Didcot.

25 North Eastern Railway J72 Class 0–6–0T, *Joem* built in 1949 and preserved at the National Railway Museum.

26 Great Western 0–6–2T, No. 6697 built in 1928 and preserved by the Great Western Society at Didcot.

27 Andrew Barclay 0–4–0CT, No. 24 *Stanton* built in Kilmarnock in 1925. The engine is seen on the Midland Railway Trust at Butterley.

28 L.M.S. Coronation Class Stanier Pacific 4–6–2, No. 6233 *Duchess of Sutherland* built at Crewe in 1928 and preserved at Bressingham in Norfolk.

29 L.M.S. Royal Scot Class 4–6–0, No. 6100 *Royal Scot* built in 1927 but depicted as rebuilt under Stanier. She is preserved at Bressingham in Norfolk.

30 Isle of Man Railway 2–4–0T, No. 5 *Mona* built by Beyer Peacock in 1874 and preserved on the Isle of Man Railway.

31 Kitson 0–6–2T, No. 29 built in 1904 and preserved on the North Yorkshire Moors Railway.

32 L.M.S. Fairburn 2–6–4T, No. 2085 built in 1951 and preserved on the Lakeside & Haverthwaite Railway.

33 L.M.S. Ivatt 1200 Class 2-6-2T, No. 41241 built in 1949 and preserved on the Keighley and Worth Valley Railway.

34 L.N.E.R. three-cylinder V2, Class 2-6-2, No. 4771 *Green Arrow* built in 1936 and preserved in the National Railway Museum.

35 Ex-South Eastern & Chatham Railway Class C 0–6–0, No. 592 built at
Longhedge in 1901 and now preserved on the Bluebell Railway.

36 Fairbourne Railway 15 in. gauge Pacific 4–6–2, *Ernest Twining* originally built by Guest of Stourbridge in 1949.

37 Ravenglass & Eskdale Railway 15 in. gauge 2–8–2, *River Mite* built by Clarkson in 1966.

Colour Plate Commentaries

1 Canterbury & Whitstable Railway 0–4–0, *Invicta*

This historic engine was built in 1830 by Robert Stephenson of Newcastle for the Canterbury & Whitstable Railway. Named *Invicta*, she was originally an 0–2–2, but was later rebuilt into an 0–4–0. Engines of the 0–4–0 wheel arrangement constituted an early form of mixed traffic and, in evolutionary terms, fell between the single wheelers and six coupled freight power. These early 0–4–0s were the antecedents of the mixed traffic 0–4–2. (See Section 7.)

2 Kitson 0–6–2T, No. 29

This engine, as an 0–6–2T, burst out of the traditional confines of the industrial locomotive. The 0–6–2T was introduced as a mixed traffic type on the coal carrying lines of South Wales between the late 1880s and mid 1920s, and when the Lambton collieries of Northumberland needed engines for duties which involved longer range operation over curved tracks, Kitson of Leeds, who had supplied 0–6–2Ts to South Wales, produced a similar type of engine. Certain main line railways adopted the 0–6–2T as a heavy shunter, whilst in the post Edwardian period the type became prevalent as a suburban engine, though in this guise the driving wheels were usually at least 5 ft. in diameter. Thus we find the 0–6–2T making an interesting cross-fertilisation of four orders; mixed traffic, shunting, industrial and suburban. (See Section 1.)

3 North Eastern Railway Class J27 0–6–0, No. 2392

The power possibilities inherent within the inside-cylinder 0–6–0 form were exploited during the Edwardian period and these engines became infinitely more pugnacious beasts. With cylinders of up to 19 in. diameter and higher boiler pressures, the engines of this period were considerably more powerful than their nineteenth century counterparts. Typical of these Edwardian designs was the North Eastern Railway's J27 Class, built for use on the slogging coal hauls as part of the company's drive to increase the power of its goods engines. The J27s were a continuation of the J26 Class introduced in 1904. (See Section 2.)

4 Lancashire and Yorkshire Railway 0–4–0ST Pug, No. 51218

The Lancashire & Yorkshire Railway built their own class of 0–4–0ST Pugs between 1891 and 1910. Their design was very similar to that of the Neilson Pugs adopted by the North British and Caledonian Railways. The L. & Y. used the engines for shunting on dockland waterfronts and for running through the streets which interconnected the various quays and loading wharfs. (See Section 5.)

97

5 L.M.S. Stanier Jubilee 4–6–0, No. 5690 *Leander*

The L.M.S.'s tradition of three-cylinder 4–6–0s which began with Fowler's Royal Scots and Patriots, was continued by Stanier with the Jubilees of which 191 were built in 1935–36. These beautiful engines—whose names celebrated Britain's greatness as a nation—were found throughout the L.M.S. system from Scotland down to South West England, and they worked many important expresses, particularly over lines where the heavier Pacifics were not allowed. (See Section 3.)

6 Norwegian State Railway Mogul 2–6–0, No. 19

Although this sprightly Norwegian Mogul 2–6–0 does not strictly belong to the British locomotive dynasty, its design was influenced by David Jones, Chief Mechanical Engineer of the Highland Railway. Jones was an adviser to the Norwegian State Railways on locomotive policy and these Moguls might be thought of as a smaller version of the Highland's Jones Goods 4–6–0s of 1894. The Norwegian Moguls were light cross country engines, similar in terms of size and power to Ivatt's 6400 Class 2–6–0s of the L.M.S. which appeared some thirty years later. (See Section 7.)

7 Southern Railway rebuilt West Country Pacific, No. 34016 *Bodmin*

The ultimate British Pacific appeared in 1956 with the rebuilding of Bulleid's Merchant Navy Class. The air-smoothed casing was removed, and traditional Walschaerts valve gear incorporated. These, along with other modifications, produced an improvement on the original design and, along with some rebuilt Light Pacifics, the type survived in main line service until 1967, by which time they were the last Pacifics to remain on heavy express passenger work. (See Section 3.)

8 G.W.R. Manor Class 4–6–0, No. 7827 *Lydham Manor*

A slightly lighter version of the Granges, which in turn were a smaller version of the Halls. The mixed traffic Manor Class 4–6–0s were designed by Collet for the G.W.R.'s secondary lines where the heavier types were forbidden, especially the former Cambrian and Midland & South Western Junction Railway systems. The first twenty Manors appeared in 1938–39, and another ten in 1950, but further building was cancelled in favour of the B.R. Standard designs. (See Section 7.)

9 Borrows 0–4–0 Well Tank type, *Windle*

Another localised concept of industrial engine is demonstrated by this 0–4–0 Well Tank, a type originally built by Borrows of St. Helens for the local glass and chemical industries. The Well Tank carries its water between the frames and, apart from being unusual amongst British industrials, was unique in having its valve gear set between the driving wheels and frames. What caused Borrows to adopt the Well Tank for these local industries is unknown and although the engines were very successful they exerted no influence upon the mainstream of development. Some sixty examples were built between 1875 and 1921, all to the same design; the type was also built by Ken Stuart of Stoke upon Trent from 1912 onwards. (See Section 1.)

10 Avonside I ft. II½ in. gauge 0–4–0T, No. 4 *Sezela*

An extensive range of 0–4–0T/0–4–2Ts was built for plantation service overseas. Apart from being easily transported, such locomotives were flexible and proved ideal for working over light and often hastily laid tracks. This 0–4–0T was exported from Bristol in 1916 for work on the Natal Sugar Estates in South Africa, and was one of a number returned to Britain for use in preserved form on I ft. II½ in. gauge lines. (See Section 4.)

II. R.S.H. 56 Class 0–6–0ST, No. 26

This huge 0–6–0ST represents a marvellous piece of evolution as despite its modern appearance it relates directly to E. B. Wilson's railway foundry in Leeds. It has already been described how R.S.H. acquired Manning Wardle's drawings and built to the original designs, but this engine is an example of R.S.H. being asked by Stewart & Lloyds Minerals at Corby to produce a bigger version of the Manning Wardle type engine illustrated on Plate 21. R.S.H. faithfully built to the original pattern and included the Haystack Firebox which has a raised top for good steamraising. The Haystack Firebox was originally designed by the railway foundry and later perpetuated by Manning Wardle, after they had procured the foundry's drawings for £48 in 1858! This engine portrays other Manning Wardle details not least in the cab design. (See Section I.)

12 Midland Railway Johnson 'Spinner' 4–2–2, No. 673

The most beautiful Single 4–2–2s ever built were undoubtedly the Johnson 'Spinners' of the Midland Railway. They appeared as late as 1887 as a principal main line express engine, and their introduction caused a brief renaissance of the Single type on other important railways, despite the ever increasing adoption of the 4–4–0. The Midland Railway continued to build these engines with detail variations until 1900, by which time the class totalled ninety-five engines. (See Section 3.)

13 Caledonian Railway Single 4–2–2, No. 123

Many people regard the graceful beauty of the Single as never having been surpassed. It was certainly a concept in which the design skills of the Victorians could be given free reign. One of the most beautiful was the solitary 4–2–2 built in 1886 by Neilsons for the Edinburgh Exhibition and subsequently taken over by the Caledonian Railway. This engine undertook some startling running between Carlisle and Edinburgh during the 1888 Railway Races to Scotland. (See Section 3.)

14 London & South Western Railway Drummond Class T9 4–4–0, No. 120

This lovely class made its appearance at the height of the inside-cylinder 4–4–0's reign as the nation's leading express passenger type. They were built between 1899 and 1901, having been designed by Drummond for the London & South Western Railway, and were of similar generic order to his earlier 4–4–0s prepared for the North British and Caledonian. Brilliant in every way, they earned the nickname Greyhounds on account of their fleet-footedness, and the last examples were not withdrawn until the early 1960s. (See Section 3.)

15 Midland Railway Kirtley 2–4–0, No. 158A

This classic engine is one of Kirtley's Midland Railway 2–4–0s with 6 ft 2½ in. diameter driving wheels. The class contained twenty-nine engines which were built between 1866 and 1874. Further 2–4–0s were built for the Midland under Johnson, and the type became an important part of the motive power roster. Though primarily a passenger design, the Kirtley engines also undertook freight work and thus were an early form of mixed traffic engine, in contrast with most 2–4–0s of the period, which were exclusively for express passenger duties. (See Section 7.)

16 Great Eastern Railway J15 Class, No. 564

One of the best known mixed traffic designs of the late nineteenth century, was Holden's Great Eastern Railway J15s. This class represents the ubiquitous inside-cylinder 0–6–0 in general duty form, as compared with the heavy freight variety. The class totalled 289 engines built between 1883 and 1913. They were true 'maids of all work', and their enduring ubiquity is demonstrated by the fact that as late as 1958 some could still be found working cross-country passenger and goods trains in East Anglia. (See Section 7.)

17 L.N.E.R. Class K1 2–6–0, No. 2005

The last class of Moguls to appear before the introduction of B.R.'s standard designs was the L.N.E.R. K1s which were developed from a Thompson rebuild of a Gresley K4. In appearance they were a smaller Mogul version of the B1, 4–6–0, but were actually more powerful by virtue of their 5 ft. 2 in. diameter wheels, compared with the B1's 6 ft. 2 in. The K1s brought the L.N.E.R.'s Mogul era to a fitting close, as they were an updated equivalent of Gresley's first G.N. K2s of 1914. The class totalled seventy engines built in 1949–50. (See Section 7.)

18 London & South Western Railway Adams 4–4–2T, No. 488

Beattie's 2–4–0WTs were replaced by seventy-one of these splendid 4–4–2Ts known as Adams Radials. All were built between 1882 and 1885. Dispersal from suburban duty began during the Edwardian period, and three ended up on the Lyme Regis branch where they survived until the line closed in 1961. (See Section 6.)

19 Southern Railway unrebuilt West Country Pacific 4–6–2, No. 21C 123
Blackmore Vale

The L.N.E.R.'s three-cylinder Pacific tradition was continued on the Southern with Bulleid's Merchant Navy Class of 1941. These engines were air-smoothed rather than streamlined, and they embodied many interesting developments aimed at perpetuating steam traction. Included were a 280 lb per sq in. boiler pressure, thermic syphons in the firebox, a chain driven valve gear completely enclosed in an oil bath, and boxpok driving wheels. The Merchant Navy's had an axle weight of 21 tons, and in 1945 Bulleid introduced a slightly smaller version which were known as the West Country and Battle of Britain Class. These engines had an 18¾ ton axle load and were allowed to go virtually anywhere on the Southern system. These Light Pacifics, as they were called, were the first to appear for more general and widespread use, rather than purely fast main line work, and in this respect they were the direct

forerunners of the British Railway's Britannia and Clan Pacifics of 1951.
(See Section 3.)

20 Neilson 0–4–0ST Pug, *Alfred Paget*

One of the early forms of small 0–4–0 Saddle Tank was the classic Scottish Pug.
Equally suited for contractors and industrial users alike, it first emerged from
Neilson's Hyde Park Works, Glasgow with Ogee type tanks. An interesting
cross-fertilisation occurred when the Neilson Pug was adopted as a standard
main line shunter by the North British Railway, and in very similar form by
the Caledonian Railway too. The term Pug was the traditional Scottish name
for a small four-wheeled shunting engine but it eventually became common
parlance for all Scottish shunting tanks. (See Section 1.)

21 Manning Wardle type 0–6–0ST, *Penn Green*

Although this 0–6–0ST was built in 1941 by Robert Stephenson & Hawthorn,
she is a classic Leeds product and a typical member of the Manning Wardle
family of industrial saddle tanks. The first engine of this type was built by
Manning Wardle for the Inland Waterways and Docks in 1917. Following
Manning Wardle's demise in 1926, their goodwill and patterns passed to
neighbouring Kitsons, but after their closure in 1938, all drawings went to
R.S.H. Both Kitson and R.S.H. continued to build to the old M.W. designs
whenever required by the company's former customers. Upon the closure of
R.S.H.'s Newcastle works in 1960, the drawings for both Kitson and M.W.
were adopted by Hunslet. This purchase returned the designs to the parish
of their birth, but sadly by this time the lineage was on the verge of extinction.
(See Section 1.)

22 L.M.S. Stanier 8F 2–8–0, No. 8233

When Stanier undertook his mighty restocking of the L.M.S. he solved all
deficiencies in the freight locomotive roster by introducing his 8F Class
2–8–0 in 1935—thirty-two years after similar engines had appeared on the
Great Western Railway! The 8Fs became the definitive British 2–8–0 and were
the heavy freight counterpart of Stanier's equally celebrated Black 5 Mixed
Traffic 4–6–0. The 8Fs lasted until the very end of steam traction in 1968.
(See Section 2.)

23 Great Northern Railway 0–6–0ST, No. 1247

For heavier shunting duties the Great Northern Railway adopted an original
0–6–0ST design of 1892 by Stirling. These engines were continued under Ivatt
and became known as the J52s; when building finished in 1909, the class
totalled over 130 engines. The J52s had 18 in. cylinders and a tractive effort
of 21,735 lbs and were powerful engines for their day. Gresley followed them
with his even more powerful J50 Class of 1922, which were essentially an
updated side tank version. (See Section 5.)

24 Great Western Railway 1361 Class 0–6–0ST, No. 1363

In 1910 Churchward introduced this class of five 0–6–0STs, with short
wheelbases for dock shunting on the Great Western system. As with most
Churchward designs, the class was extended under Collet, and in 1934 more
examples appeared but in the guise of Pannier Tanks. These engines were

considerably lighter than the G.W.'s standard 0–6–0PT shunters and in their later years could be seen working Channel Islands Boat Trains through the streets of Weymouth to the quayside. (See Section 5.)

25 North Eastern Railway J72 Class 0–6–0T, *Joem*

This class of 0–6–0Ts was designed by Wilson Worsdell, Chief Mechanical Engineer on the North Eastern Railway. The first twenty engines were built at Darlington in 1898–99, and at that time no one could have imagined that building would continue intermittently over a fifty-three year period! Nevertheless, these engines were built under three administrations, the N.E.R., L.N.E.R. and British Railways. The class finally totalled 113 engines and some survived until the mid 1960s. No other instance exists in British locomotive history of a class being built virtually unchanged over a period of more than half a century. This remarkable occurrence underlines the conservatism which characterised the typical main line shunter over a seventy-five year period. (See Section 5.)

26 Great Western 0–6–2T, No. 6697

The 0–6–2T appeared in several guises, but in South Wales it was an important mixed traffic engine, both on the G.W.R. and on its Welsh constituents, such as the Taff Vale and Rhymney Railways. From the late nineteenth century, 0–6–2Ts were used amid the Welsh Valleys for working local passenger, coal hauls and shunting. This class represented the last manifestation of the type, and was introduced by Collet in 1924, immediately after the grouping; building continued until 1928, by which time the class totalled two hundred engines. They survived amid the valleys of South Wales until the mid 1960s— three quarters of a century after the 0–6–2T first appeared there. (See Section 7.)

27 Andrew Barclay 0–4–0CT, No. 24 *Stanton*

The Crane Engine was a logical adaptation of the small shunting tank. It found favour in yards where heavy materials needed to be picked up and loaded as part of the shunting operation. First introduced by the London & North Western Railway in 1866, a wide variety of engines subsequently appeared both for industrial and main line owners. Lifting capacities ranged from two to five tons and the most prolific builder was Andrew Barclay. Crane Tanks were never employed as widely as might have been expected, and came a poor second to the more conventional types of yard crane. The advent of mobile diesel cranes and heavy duty fork-lift trucks led to the crane engine's further demise and ultimate extinction. (See Section 1.)

28 L.M.S. Coronation Class Stanier Pacific 4–6–2, No. 6233
Duchess of Sutherland

Following the success of Stanier's Princess Royals, an improved version appeared in 1937 with the streamlined Coronation Class. These engines were the L.M.S.'s equivalent of the L.N.E.R. A4, and on test in 1937 No. 6220 *Coronation* reached the unprecedented speed of 114 mph, only to be beaten by *Mallard* one year later. During its test run, *Coronation* covered the 158 miles from Crewe–London (Euston) in 118 minutes, an average speed of 80 mph. The last of the Coronations did not appear until 1947, by which time the class totalled thirty-nine engines. Not all were streamlined. Stanier's two classes of Pacific remained in charge of the top duties over the West Coast Main Line until displaced by diesels during the early 1960s. (See Section 3.)

29 L.M.S. Royal Scot Class 4–6–0, No. 6100 *Royal Scot*
In 1927, the same year that the Kings appeared on the Great Western, the L.M.S., who operated a far greater range of express passenger services, introduced the three-cylinder Royal Scot Class—which were much less powerful engines! Nevertheless, these three-cylinder 4–6–0s represented a considerable advance over the earlier Claughton 4–6–0s, and brought about a considerable improvement in passenger services. (See Section 3.)

30 Isle of Man Railway 2–4–0T, No. 5 *Mona*
The 2–4–0T and related 4–4–0T, became prevalent from the mid nineteenth century onwards as medium sized engines with good stability for work over secondary tracks. These Isle of Man Railway 2–4–0Ts are one of a whole family of similar engines built by Beyer Peacock of Manchester for various gauges. The immediate forerunner of these Isle of Man engines was a 3 ft 6 in. gauge 2–4–0T, built by Beyer Peacock for Norway in 1870, whilst similar locomotives were prepared for the Ballymena and Larne Railway in 1880. The Isle of Man 2–4–0Ts embodied some classic Beyer Peacock features such as bell mouthed domes, salter safety valves, wheel-type smoke box door handles, a shapely chimney with thick lips and curvacious splashers. In all, a pedigree for some highly attractive locomotives. (See Section 4.)

31 Kitson 0–6–2T, No. 29—See commentary for Plate 2.

32 L.M.S. Fairburn 2–6–4T, No. 2085
The antecedents of these magnificent engines date back to 1927 when Fowler introduced his 2300 Class, 2–6–4Ts. The 2–6–4T constituted the ultimate suburban type and it was continued in modified form by Stanier from 1935 onwards, and later by Fairburn. These three types provided the L.M.S. with an excellent all round tank for suburban and branch passenger duties. They became extremely widespread, except for Stanier's three-cylinder variety which was confined to the former London Tilbury & Southend Railway's lines between Fenchurch Street and Shoeburyness. These engines adequately fulfilled the dreams to which Whitelegge had aspired when he introduced the massive 4–6–2Ts onto the line in 1912. (See Section 6.)

33 L.M.S. Ivatt 1200 Class 2–6–2T, No. 41241
The L.M.S. also developed a lineage of 2–6–2Ts which ran counter to the previously mentioned 2–6–4Ts. These also began with Fowler and were continued by Stanier. However, under Ivatt a smaller version was produced in 1946 with the 1200 Class. Many were motor fitted for working 'push and pull' trains on branch lines and apart from being widespread on the L.M.S. system, also appeared on the north-eastern and southern regions. In common with the Fairburn 2–6–4Ts, these engines provided the basis for one of the B.R. standard designs—in this case the 84000 Class of 1953. (See Section 6.)

34 L.N.E.R. three-cylinder V2 Class 2–6–2, No. 4771 *Green Arrow*
This stalwart of British locomotive history is one of Gresley's three-cylinder
V2 2–6–2s which appeared in 1936 for heavy mixed traffic work throughout
the L.N.E.R. system. The V2s achieved initial fame in working the famous
3/35 Scottish goods from Kings Cross. Gresley favoured the Mogul and 2–6–2
types for mixed traffic duties, and in 1941 he produced his three-cylinder V4
2–6–2, a lightweight version of the V2. Intended as a new mixed traffic design,
only two V4s were built as Thompson, following Gresley's death, adopted the
two-cylinder 4–6–0 in common with the other railways, and in 1942, his
first B1s were put into traffic. (See Section 7.)

35 Ex-South Eastern & Chatham Railway Class C 0–6–0
Part of the fascination of locomotive history is the glorious diversity of
designs which evolved under the private railway companies. Although many
of the different engines produced varied little in essential details, each bore
the characteristics of its designer and had a distinct individuality. This is the
South Eastern & Chatham Railways Class C inside-cylinder 0–6–0, one of
109 engines built between 1900 and 1908. Though primarily freight engines,
the Cs became celebrated for their competence in hauling passenger trains.
(See Section 2.)

36 Fairbourne Railway 15 in. gauge Pacific 4–6–2, *Ernest Twining*
This engine was originally built as a 15 in. miniature gauge Black 5 for the
Dudley Zoo Railway, by Guest of Stourbridge. In 1966 she was rebuilt into a
Pacific with British colonial pretensions, and now works on the Fairbourne
Railway. The engine is a representative of the Greenly school of practice.
(See Section 4.)

37 Ravenglass & Eskdale Railway 15 in. gauge 2–8–2, *River Mite*
Another member of the Greenly genus is *River Mite*, a Clarkson 2–8–2 of 1966.
This handsome engine works on the Ravenglass and Eskdale Railway which
was the first complete line to absorb the three miniature locomotive building
traditions of Bassett-Lowke, Greenly and Heywood. (See Section 4.)

SECTION 5

Shunting Engines

Half a century was to pass between the appearance of Trevithick's first locomotive in 1804 and the main line shunting engine as we know it. During that period, the evolutionary niche had not occurred for such an order of locomotives. Although the main line railway spread rapidly from 1825 onwards, there was a considerable time lapse before the various companies joined up to create a cohesive network, and during this early period the main line engines of the day undertook whatever station and yard movements were necessary; but the expanding network led to rapid developments in locomotive design, and by 1850 many 'obsolete' types were available for downgrading as shunters. Such engines were invariably cumbersome and quite unsuited to the task once yard traffic began to increase and during the 1860s instances occurred of main line companies buying 'off the peg' industrial designs from the private builders. The Midland Railway's adoption of Manning Wardle 0-6-0STs is one example of this.

By the late 1860s, the railway—apart from assuming the dominant role in transport—had accelerated the industrial revolution to previously unimaginable proportions. The national network was taking shape, traffic increased accordingly, stations—especially junction ones—became busy and the formation of trains ever more complex; goods yards and exchange sidings became an integral part of the railway. By this time the main line engines were becoming too large and specialised for adapting to shunting, whilst 'off the peg' industrials were not only too small for the heavier yard shunts but the railway companies preferred to build their own locomotives to the designs of their Chief Mechanical Engineers. Thus came the demand for a special order of engines to fulfil the subordinate yet vital role of shunting.

Once again, the 0-6-0 offered the necessary power and adhesion and the tank type, either side or saddle, was chosen. Such engines were easily mobile for moving backwards and forwards and, as in the case of the industrial, the weight of the fuel bearing directly onto the driving

North London Railway 0–6–0T No. 2650 built at Bow Works, London, in 1880 and preserved on the Bluebell Railway. The North London Railway chose the 0–6–0T as the basis for their standard class of shunting engine and thirty were built at the company's Bow Works between 1879 and 1905. Their

tractive-effort of 18,140 lbs was typical of the main line shunter and apart from performing shunting duties, these engines worked small local freights. This locomotive is the only survivor from the North London Railway.

North Eastern Railway Y7 Class 0–4–0T, built in 1891 and preserved on the Middleton Railway, Leeds. The shunting locomotive order includes a family of small four-coupled types with very short wheelbases for negotiating the tight curves found in docks and workshops. Such engines are epitomised by this North Eastern Railway Y7 Class 0–4–0T which was one of twenty-four engines built between 1888 and 1923. Unlike many of its relations, this engine has inside cylinders.

wheels provided valuable adhesion for moving long lines of wagons. Indeed, tender engines offered no advantage as only limited amounts of coal was needed for yard work, and water could easily be taken between bouts of shunting.

One of the earliest and most important examples of a main line shunter was Ramsbottom's 'Special' 0-6-0ST built for the London & North Western Railway during the 1860s. This railway operated many mineral trains and served a wide range of industrial areas. The type was continued by F. W. Webb from 1871 onwards and became the principal shunting engine for the entire L. & N.W.R. network. Another distinctive family of early shunters appeared on the industrial belt of Scotland when Neilson introduced their celebrated 0-4-0ST 'Pug'. Initially these were built for industrial users, but they appeared on several main line companies, including the Great Eastern Railway, who in 1874 designed a version with Ogee type tanks.

After 1875, however, the main line shunting engine progressed as an entirely separate order of locomotives quite distinct from its industrial ancestors. Although many earlier designs were saddle tanks, the side tank became generally preferred not least on the Midland when Johnson introduced his first 0-6-0T for shunting in 1874. No less than 280 had been built by 1899, after which the type evolved into his famous Jinty 0-6-0T, sixty of which were built between 1899 and 1902.

On the Great Western, both Swindon and Wolverhampton built large numbers of 0-6-0STs during the last quarter of the nineteenth century, but from 1904 onwards many underwent rebuilding and the saddle tanks were replaced by a separate oblong shaped variety, slung either side of the boiler and appropriately known as panniers. Thus was born the type of shunting engine for which the G.W. was renowned throughout the remainder of its existence.

Whatever the type of tank, the 0-6-0 reigned supreme and numerous designs, delightfully varied in their appearance but almost identical in power output, appeared over the late Victorian and Edwardian period. Notable examples include the Great Eastern Railway's J67 Class 0-6-0Ts of which 160 were built between 1886 and 1904, and Ivatt's Great Northern 0-6-0STs, J52 Class, of which 137 engines were built between 1892 and 1909.

By the Edwardian period, shunting had become a complex operation; trains were longer, more frequent and invariably comprised of wagons bound for many destinations. Considerable thought had to be given to the design and layout of marshalling yards, and some of the larger ones adopted the hump system whereby wagons were pushed uncoupled up an incline and allowed to roll by gravity down the other side and on into whichever siding was appropriate. Obviously such yards demanded something much more potent than an 0-6-0 tank, and consequently a small but fascinating family of shunting engines known as 'humpers' evolved.

The first of these giants appeared in 1907 when Robinson introduced a three-cylinder 0-8-4T for humping at the Great Central's Wath Yards, whilst two years later the ever prolific Wilson Worsdell C.M.E. of the North Eastern put into traffic some three-cylinder 4-8-0Ts. The L. & N.W.R. introduced the first of thirty 0-8-2Ts in 1911 followed by an equal number of 0-8-4Ts. These two classes were in effect a heavy shunting version of their standard 0-8-0 freight engines. The London & South Western Railway also developed the 4-8-0T for humping at Feltham Yards, but these engines were of a

Port Talbot Railway 0–6–0ST, No. 813 built in 1900 by Hudswell Clarke of Leeds and preserved on the Severn Valley Railway. This fascinating engine was one of six 0–6–0STs built by Hudswell Clarke of Leeds for the Port Talbot Railway in 1900. The engine had 16 in. cylinders and 4 ft diameter driving wheels. Following the absorption of the Port Talbot Railway into the Great Western, the engine became 'Swindonised' by receiving a G.W. boiler, and is thus a fascinating cross relationship between two classic schools of design, those of Leeds and Swindon: a truly rare locomotive.

much more modern design with two outside cylinders and Walschaerts valve gear.

The hump shunter's radical departure from the 0–6–0 was totally eclipsed by the banking engine which at its extreme aspired to unbelievable limits. Although banking engines belong to a different order, similarities exist with the humper, and they can be mentioned in passing. The first instance occurred in 1919 when the Midland Railway produced a four-cylinder 0–10–0 for banking over the Lickey Incline with its continuous three miles of 1 in 37; but the ultimate in power came in 1925 when the L.N.E.R.'s six-cylinder 2–8–0 + 0–8–2 Garratt appeared for banking over the Worsboro' Incline near Wath.

With a tractive-effort of some 73,000 lbs this brontosaurus was equivalent to a pair of three-cylinder Gresley 2-8-os.

These thrills represented but a phase and the conventional 0-6-0 continued to work on all but the very heaviest of shunting duties. Following the grouping, the L.M.S. built over four hundred more Midland Railway Jinties, but even more dramatic was the G.W.s 5700 Class 0-6-0PTs which from 1929 grew to a staggering total of 863 engines. It must be mentioned, however, that the 5700 Class were sometimes used for local goods and branch passenger work. In all, the G.W.R. built some 2,400 0-6-0 shunting tanks.

Despite the profligacy of certain types following the grouping, the shunting engine as a specialised design concept went into rapid decline after 1930. It was on shunting duties that the first diesel inroads were made into steam's monopoly, for the diesel with its capacity to switch on and off for work which often involved long periods of idleness, showed a clear advantage. Furthermore, its even torque provided sure footed starts with heavy loads, whilst its easy man-oeuvrability was another advantage. Commensurate with the advent of diesel shunters came the inevitable rundown of countless moderately sized inside-cylinder 0-6-0s of Victorian origin. These had either been superseded by larger engines, or were simply too old to be employed on the heavier and more demanding schedules of the day. Vast numbers of these engines made a natural gravitation into the shunting yards.

On the L.M.S. network former goods engines from the L. & N.W.R., Midland, and Caledonian fulfilled extensive shunting duties for the remainder of the Company's existence. A similar situation existed on the L.N.E.R. and after the last of Gresley's J50 0-6-0Ts had been built in 1937 no new shunting engines were designed. On the Southern Railway extensive electrification had released numerous small tank engines formerly used on suburban and local passenger work, and these were relegated to shunting.

World War Two created a brief renaissance in shunting design when in 1943 the Hunslet Austerity 0-6-0ST was specially produced for military operations. Following the war, those surplus to military requirements were sold, and although many went to collieries seventy-five were taken by the L.N.E.R. as shunters in 1946 and classified J94. This was another example of cross-fertilisation similar to the one which had occurred seventy-five years earlier with the Neilson Pugs.

South Eastern and Chatham Railway P Class 0-6-0T, No. 27 built in 1910 and preserved on the Bluebell Railway. This diminutive engine once belonged to a class of eight. Although looking very much like shunting engines they were originally intended for working light passenger trains over branch lines. They

proved unsuitable for these duties, however, and were predictably relegated to shunting and shed pilot work. Designed by Wainwright for the South Eastern & Chatham Railway in 1909, they were remarkably small and had 12 in. cylinders and a tractive-effort of only 7,810 lbs, weighing a mere 28 tons.

L.M.S. 0-6-0T Jinty, No. 16440, built in 1926 and preserved at the Midland Railway Centre, Butterley. This Midland Railway engine represents the culmination of one of the finest families of shunting tank in locomotive history. The lineage began in 1874 when Johnson introduced a smaller version of the engine shown and built some 280 examples. In 1899 he followed these with sixty engines of a slightly larger design, and these formed the basis for the

celebrated Jinties of which a total of 422 were built under the L.M.S. between 1924 and 1931. During their fifty-eight year period of evolution, Midland Railway 0–6–0Ts progressed from 17 to 18 in. cylinder diameters, from 140 lbs to 160 lbs in boiler pressure, and from 15,000 lbs to 20,800 lbs in tractive effort. Engine weights advanced from thirty-nine to forty-nine tons. In all, this genera totalled 762 engines.

L.N.E.R. 4WVBTG Class Y1 Sentinel built in 1933 by the Sentinel Wagon Works, Shrewsbury and preserved on the Middleton Railway in Leeds. The L.N.E.R. made a departure from conventional practice in 1925 when they purchased the first of several batches of 4WVBTGs from the Sentinel Wagon Works in Shrewsbury. Intended for light dock shunting, these extremely small engines had geared transmission and their cylinders of only 6¾ in. diameter were capable of generating a tractive-effort—where low gears were fitted—of 15,960 lbs. This was extremely high considering that the Sentinel's weight was only 20 tons. This compares extremely well with the Neilson Pug which weighed some 27 tons for a tractive-effort of only 9,845 lbs! However, whatever advantages the Sentinel appeared to offer, it exerted no influence as a main line shunter in Britain and remained confined to a handful of classes. These tended to appear on Departmental duties rather than on main line shunting work proper.

United States Army Transportation Corps 0–6–0T, No. 72, built by the
Vulcan Iron Works in 1943, and preserved on the Keighley and Worth Valley
Railway. This typical American design has no place in the evolution of the
British shunting engine as such, except that it was a standard design for the
United States Army Transportation Corps during World War Two. Most
worked outside the United Kingdom, but fourteen were purchased by the
Southern Railway in 1946. However, the design's modern proportions and
outside valve gear almost certainly influenced the design of the last British
main line shunting engine, the G.W.R.'s 1500 Class of 1949.

Hunslet Austerity 0–6–0ST, No. 26 *Linda* built by Hunslet of Leeds in 1952, and preserved on the Kent & East Sussex Railway. The Hunslet Austerity is one of the classic shunting locomotives of all time. First introduced by Hunslet of Leeds in 1943 for the Ministry of Supply during World War Two, the type was built over a twenty-one year period and eventually reached a grand total of 484 engines. The Hunslet Austerity was most prolific on the National Coal Board upon which it became the standard type although seventy-five engines were adopted by the L.N.E.R. in 1946 from surplus War Department stocks. These engines took the classification J94.

Below

A fascinating mixture of shunters, with Norwegian State Railway Nohab Mogul 2–6–0, No. 19 (second from the right), preserved on the Kent and East Sussex Railway, which re-opened in 1974. They comprise three Hunslet Austerity 0–6–0ST engines (extreme right, and third and fourth from left), an R.S.H. 56 Class 0–6–0ST (extreme left), two 0–6–0T Terrier Class engines (second from left, and fifth from right), a Peckett 0–4–0T (fourth from right), and a Manning Wardle 0–6–0ST (third from right).

The War also left fourteen of the standard United States Army Transportation Corps 0-6-0Ts in Britain and these were taken by the Southern Railway in 1946, and set to work shunting in Southampton Docks.

It fell to the Great Western to formally end the order with their 1500 Class/9400 Class 0-6-0PT heavy shunters designed by Hawksworth. Originally intended as a new standard class for the G.W.R., only ten 1500s were built and they appeared in 1949—one year after nationalisation. The first 9400 Class appeared in 1947 and building continued right through until 1956, by which time the class totalled 210 engines. These were the last engines of pre-nationalisation design to be built under British Railways.

However, it must be mentioned that the British shunting engine ended with an incredible evolutionary flourish when in 1950—two years after nationalisation—British Railways suddenly built twenty-eight 0-6-0Ts to a nineteenth century design! The engines concerned had been designed by Worsdell for the North Eastern Railway in 1898 and under the L.N.E.R. had been classified J72. Furthermore, the J72s were merely a modified version of Worsdell's J71s of 1886! This amazing action was all the more remarkable when one considers that diesels were, by this time, clearly accepted as the shunting engine of the future. It would be very difficult to think of any other locomotive design in world history which had been built over a fifty-three year period without alteration.

This magnificent story ended an entire order of locomotives. Under the standard designs set out by British Railways in 1951—the year that the last J72 was built—no shunting engines were included. The golden years had been between 1875 and 1930, and amid the great diversity of Saddle, Side and Pannier tanks built, the overall power output had been remarkably similar, expanding but slightly over successive decades.

SECTION 6

Engines for Suburban, Branch Lines and Cross Country Services

The expansion of cities under the industrial revolution created a pattern of urban living which was becoming widely established by the middle of the nineteenth century. The subsequent need for frequent and rapid communications gave birth to the suburban steam train. This aspect of railway operation hastened a change in the entire pattern of British society, by providing easy and rapid travel from home to place of work, and thus enabling commerce to become centralised within the cities.

Suburban engines were almost exclusively tank designs as the absence of a tender facilitated ease of running in either direction and saved the cumbersome and time consuming business of turning. Furthermore, the weight of the water over the coupled wheels provided useful adhesion for making rapid starts from stations.

London's suburbs were an obvious spawning ground for the new order, which began dramatically in 1864 with the Metropolitan tanks, an extremely handsome class of 4-4-0Ts with 5 ft. 9 in. diameter driving wheels. These engines were fitted with condensing apparatus for working underground on both the Metropolitan and District railways. Designed and built by Beyer Peacock of Manchester, 120 were shared by the two lines and the engines remained at work until displaced by electrification in 1905.

Commensurate with the appearance of Beyer Peacock's 4-4-0Ts for the underground, came the Beattie 2-4-0 Well Tanks for suburban services on the London & South Western Railway from Waterloo. This class was also built by Beyer Peacock and it heralded the first of three distinct generations of suburban engines on services from Waterloo. The second generation appeared during the 1880s when Adam's larger 4-4-2Ts took over. These survived until the late 1890s, after which Drummond's celebrated M7, 0-4-4Ts, began to appear and large batches survived until electrification. In contrast, the suburban runs over the London, Brighton & South Coast Railway from Victoria were worked from 1872 onwards by Stroudley's famous

Below

Metropolitan Railway Condensing 4-4-0T, No. 23 built by Beyer Peacock in 1866 and preserved in the London Transport Museum. The suburban steam locomotive evolved dramatically in 1864 with these 4-4-0Ts designed and built by Beyer Peacock for use on London's Metropolitan and later District railways. The type was also adopted in small numbers by the Midland, L. & N.W.R., and L. & S.W.R. Typically Beyer Peacock, they formed part of a larger group of identifiably similar tank engines built as 2-4-0s and 4-4-0s.

Right

London Brighton & South Coast Railway 0-6-0T 'Terrier', No. 10 *Sutton* built in 1876 and preserved on the Kent & East Sussex Railway. The antecedents of these famous engines were a class of similar 0-6-0Ts which Stroudley introduced for the Highland Railway in 1869. Following his appointment as C.M.E. of the London Brighton & South Coast Railway, he introduced the first of these 'Terriers' in 1872, and fifty were built over an eight year period. As suburban engines, they are unusual in having only coupled axles. After displacement on working suburban trains out of Victoria, they became widely dispersed and gravitated to branch lines, shunting and even industrial service in collieries. They provide a perfect example of a downgraded suburban engine finding alternative work of a diverse nature.

METROPOLITAN ... LOCOMOTIVE Nº 23.1866   METROPOLITAN RAILWAY LOCOMOTIVE Nº 23.1866

London & South Western Railway Beattie 2–4–0WT Class 0298, No. E0314 built in 1874 and preserved at Quainton. The 2–4–0WT made its appearance as a suburban engine with this design in 1863. Eighty-eight were built for the L. & S.W.R.'s services based upon London Waterloo. They were extremely small engines and following their replacement by 4–4–2Ts during the 1880s they were either rebuilt into 2–4–0 tender engines or withdrawn. All had disappeared by 1899 except three which found favour on a mineral branch line in North Cornwall, where they survived 'frozen in time' for over sixty years and were not withdrawn until 1962—almost one century after their sisters began working out of Waterloo!

0-6-0T Terriers; followed one year later by his D Class 0-4-2Ts.

Another important class appeared when the North London Railway introduced their 4-4-0Ts in 1868; these were followed in 1869 by the first of a long line of 0-4-4Ts on the Midland Railway. It will be noted that during this first decade many permutations were played on the four-coupled theme, for the suburban engine, unlike goods and shunting engines, evolved in a wide variety of forms, although up to the Edwardian period the 0-4-4T might be regarded as the definitive type.

Apart from its excellent flexibility for running in either direction, the 0-4-4T's boiler and cylinder blocks were often interchangeable with sister inside-cylinder 0-6-0s—if not inside-cylinder 4-4-0 express passenger engines too! Important railways which used the 0-4-4T, apart from the Midland and L. & S.W.R., included the Caledonian, North British, North Eastern, South Eastern & Chatham, London-Brighton & South Coast, and the Metropolitan. Other railways adopted the 2-4-2T, notably the London & North Western and Lancashire & Yorkshire, though perhaps the most prolific user was the Great Eastern for its extensive services from London Liverpool Street.

Evolution took a remarkable step forward in 1886 when nine massive 0-6-4Ts fitted with condensing apparatus were built for the underground railway between Liverpool and Birkenhead. At the time of their inception these were the largest engines in Britain. However, their life on suburban workings was destined to be short and they were displaced by electrification during the early years of the century.

Paradoxically it was electrification—or rather the threat of it—which gave rise to the most remarkable suburban engine imaginable, when Holden produced his Decapod 0-10-0T for the Great Eastern in 1902. The advocates of electrification claimed that a 315 ton train could be accelerated to 30 mph in 30 seconds, and in producing this epic Holden proved that such achievement could be bettered with steam. As a result, the proposed electrification of the G.E.s suburban services from Liverpool Street was shelved. Unfortunately, the Decapod was extremely heavy on the track and did not actually go into service.

As the population of Britain's large cities increased, so likewise did the proportions of the suburban tank which, from the Edwardian period, graduated to the 4-4-2T, especially on the London Tilbury &

London Brighton & South Coast Railway Class E4 0–6–2T, No. 473 *Birch Grove* built in 1898 and preserved on the Bluebell Railway. The London Brighton & South Coast Railway was an early user of the 0–6–2T suburban type, and they introduced these engines, classified E4, in 1897. The class had

5 ft. diameter driving wheels and heralded the E5, 0–6–2Ts of 1902 which had larger 5 ft. 6 in. diameter wheels. After being displaced by the electrification of lines from Victoria the E4s/E5s gravitated to branch lines and shunting duties. Examples of both classes survived into British Railway's ownership.

Southend, London Brighton & South Coast, Great Northern, Great Central and North British. Both the 0-4-4T and 4-4-2T, provided an excellent basis for extremely balanced design proportions and many highly attractive engines resulted. However, the *pièce de résistance* in sheer aesthetical terms was reached with the 4-4-4T—the ultimate in balanced proportions! Although the first 4-4-4T appeared on the Wirral Railway in 1896, it was a concept of the Edwardian period and the best known examples worked on the Metropolitan Railway. These engines vied with the Great Central Atlantics in terms of sheer beauty. The 4-4-4T also appeared on the North Eastern Railways; sadly, no examples of this lovely wheel arrangement have been preserved.

The post-Edwardian period led to larger six-coupled traction on the suburban workings of many railways. Apart from the commuting public's needs, railway traffic was by this time extremely heavy and a

South Eastern & Chatham Railway Class H 0-4-4T, No. 263 built at Ashford in 1905 and preserved on the Bluebell Railway. This late design of 0-4-4T was introduced by Wainwright for the South Eastern & Chatham Railway in 1904, and sixty-six locomotives were built up to 1915. Electrification forced many to rural retreats throughout Kent, Surrey and Sussex, although some remained around London for shunting and working empty stock trains. Almost all passed into British Railway's ownership, and the last was not withdrawn until the early 1960s.

suburban train fitted in ahead of an express could not be allowed to drag its heels. Despite this, the suburban locomotive was never under the avid pressures applied to the express passenger engine; indeed many local platforms were too short to accommodate long trains. If the incessant demand for more speed and power dictated the development of the express passenger locomotive, it was the ability to operate lively and frequent services which dominated the suburban engine's evolution.

Having said this, the post Edwardian phases of suburban engines were intended for heavier trains caused in part by an increase in the weight of coaching stock. The next evolutionary stage from the 0–4–4T was the 0–6–2T, which had first appeared as a purely suburban engine on the London Brighton & South Coast Railway in 1897 with the E4 Class; these were followed by the extremely fast moving E5s in 1902. The two most celebrated 0–6–2T designs were the Great

Great Western Railway 4500 Class 2–6–2T, No. 4566 built in 1924 and preserved on the Severn Valley Railway. A compact and efficient class of branch line engines introduced by Churchward for the Great Western in 1906. Building continued until 1929 to a total of 175 engines. This standard class worked throughout the Great Western system and remained a principal branch line type virtually until the end of steam.

London Tilbury & Southend Railway Class 79, 4–4–2T, No. 80 *Thundersley* built in 1909 and preserved at Bressingham. The 4–4–2T was an extremely elegant basis for a locomotive and the type appeared extensively as a suburban design between 1880 and 1920. One of the finest genus of 4–4–2T was on the London Tilbury and Southend Railway, who made extensive use of the type

for their services from Fenchurch Street. The first appeared in 1880, and the last one was not built until 1930, long after the L.T. & S.R. had disappeared as a separate entity. Three basic types of 4–4–2T evolved on the L.T. & S.R., Small, Intermediate and Large, and this engine belongs to the last group having been built in 1909.

Great Western Railway Churchward/Collet 6100 Class 2-6-2T, No. 6106 built in 1931 and preserved by the Great Western Society at Didcot. The Great Western adopted the 2-6-2T from the early years of this century with separate designs for suburban and branch work. In common with G.W. practice the first suburban 2-6-2Ts introduced by Churchward in 1903 were

continued by Collet with his 6100 Class. Only detail differences occurred, although the new engines did have a higher boiler pressure. A total of seventy Collet 6100 Class 2–6–2T locomotives was built between 1931 and 1935, and they were extensively used on the heavy suburban runs in the London area.

Great Western Railway 1400 Class 0–4–2T, No. 1466 built in 1936 and preserved by the Great Western Society, Didcot. This interesting class of 0–4–2Ts constituted a modern version of an original design which dated back to 1868, and is another example of the Great Western building updated engines to traditional designs. Seventy-five were built between 1932 and 1936,

and they replaced their predecessors on country branch line trains. In all, the G.W.R. had 240 0–4–2Ts and they proved excellent for working two-coach 'push and pull' services at lively speeds in the golden days when branch lines were an integral part of the nation's transport system. The batch built in the 1930s were classified 4800.

Eastern N7s introduced in 1914 for the suburban services out of Liverpool Street, and the Great Northern N2s of 1920 for similar duties radiating from Kings Cross. These engines were a development of the N1, 0-6-2Ts, of 1907. The N7s took over from the earlier 2-4-2Ts and performed an almost impossible task in keeping the dense suburban traffic out of Liverpool Street on the move. In this respect they were aided by a driving wheel diameter of 4 ft. 10 in. which enabled rapid starts, but led to an inevitable thrashing.

Rather less known, but even more potent, were Robinson's 4-6-2Ts first built for the Great Central in 1911. This wheel arrangement was the next logical stage from the 4-4-4T and it heralded the eight massive 4-6-4Ts of the London Tilbury and Southend Railway which appeared the following year.

After the 1923 grouping, the advent of electrification caused a steady decline in steam suburban services, and on the Southern no new examples were built. Furthermore, the suburban tank engine as a separate concept began to give way to the medium range mixed traffic engine, equally suited for cross country and branch line work. Such engines are epitomised by the long succession of 2-6-2T/2-6-4Ts built by the L.M.S. from 1927 onwards, and later by Thompson's 2-6-4Ts for the L.N.E.R. Indeed it may be said that the last pure suburban engines built were Gresley's three-cylinder V1/V3 2-6-2Ts of 1930; these were used in north-east England and Scotland where they replaced the ex-North British 4-4-2Ts. Following nationalisation all new designs were of the mixed traffic type, and these engines covered whatever steam suburban services remained.

The suburban engine has always been closely associated with branch lines. Many of Britain's branches were not built until towards the end of the nineteenth century, and they formed a perfect niche for past generations of suburban engines, some of which had been designed with branch line services in mind. Even if these engines were small and rather worn out, the pace on many rural branches was infinitely less demanding than the intense to and fro activities around the cities. Such engines were often joined by demoted express passenger designs such as early singles, 2-4-0s, and, in the later years, 4-4-0s as well. Inside-cylinder 0-6-0s, especially those which tended towards being mixed traffic engines, were also widely engaged on branch line service, as typified by the ubiquitous J15s introduced onto the Great Eastern Railway in 1883. In absolute contrast were the 4-4-2Ts built by the rurally based Midland & Great Northern Railway for its branch/cross country services. These instances give an insight into the true nature of motive power for branch lines—simply that virtually anything of modest proportions could, and did, work them.

In the years following the grouping a plethora of displaced suburban tanks could be seen in branch line service. The Southern used M7

Great Western Railway Class 6400, 0–6–0PT built in 1937 and preserved on the Dart Valley Railway. An 'intermediate' design of 0–6–0PT introduced by Collet in 1932 and incorporating Classes 5400, 6400 and 7400. The 5400/6400 series were motor fitted for 'push and pull' operation, and the 5400s possessed 5 ft. 2 in. diameter driving wheels compared with the 4 ft. 7½ in. of the others. The G.W.R. made many subtle variations upon the 0–6–0PT theme, and produced engines which were superficially identical in appearance for duties as disparate as light branch line passengers and heavy shunting.

Left
Great Western Railway 'Dukedog' 4–4–0, No. 3217 *Earl of Berkeley*, built in 1938 and preserved on the Bluebell Railway. One of the most interesting hybridisations in locomotive history occurred with these Great Western 'Dukedog' 4–4–0s. Though archaic in appearance they were introduced as recently as 1936 and incorporated the frames of older Bulldog 4–4–0s, plus the boiler and cab of the earlier Duke 4–4–0s. This new class was conceived for branch line and cross country services and many of the twenty-nine built worked on the former Cambrian system in North Wales.

Below
L.M.S. Fairburn 2–6–4T, No. 2085, built in 1951 and preserved on the Lakeside and Haverthwaite Railway. The Fairburn 2–6–4Ts represented the culmination of a succession of 2–6–2T/2–6–4Ts by Fowler, Stanier and Fairburn for the L.M.S.

British Railway's Standard 2–6–4T, No. 80079 built in 1954 and preserved on the Severn Valley Railway. The ultimate in British 2–6–4Ts were the 80000 Class introduced in 1951 under the B.R. standardisation scheme. Though officially designated mixed traffic, these engines were the direct descendants of the Stanier/Fairburn 2–6–4Ts of the L.M.S. which in turn were descended from Fowler's parallel boiler 2–6–4T of 1927. The 80000s were a finely

balanced engine, and had a cylinder diameter of 18 in., 5 ft. 8 in. diameter driving wheels, and a boiler pressure of 225 lbs. Their tractive-effort of 25,100 lbs ensured an excellent power output and the class performed well in many parts of Britain, especially in Scotland and over the former lines of the L.B.S.C.R. and L.T.S.R.

o-4-4Ts, 'Terrier' o-6-oTs and E4/5 o-6-2Ts, and the L.M.S. utilised former Midland o-4-4Ts and L.N.W.R. 2-4-2Ts, whilst the L.N.E.R. employed many G.E.R. 2-4-2Ts and G.N.R. 4-4-2Ts—to mention but a few examples. In many cases these 'adapted types' survived until their lines were either closed or dieselised, although some were replaced by the emergent mixed traffic designs—particularly from nationalisation onwards.

On the Great Western system the evolution of suburban and branch line engines was far better defined than on other railways. As far back as 1868 the company built a class of small o-4-2 tank engines specifically for branch line work, and this grew to a total of 165 engines by the end of the century. The Great Western had many branch and cross country lines but little in the way of suburban operation, and when Church-ward took office in 1903, he augmented the o-4-2Ts with two classes of 2-6-2Ts. First came his 4100s for heavier branch line and suburban work, followed in 1906 by his smaller 4500s for general branch line duties. Both classes were more powerful than the o-4-2Ts, thus three tangible levels of power output were available. Churchward's use of the 2-6-2T was years ahead of its adoption by other railways.

After Collett succeeded Churchward in 1921, these basic designs were continued and they lasted the G.W.R. for the remainder of its existence. Collett did, however, add a larger version of the 4100, when in 1931 he introduced his 6100 Class 2-6-2Ts with 5 ft. 8 in. diameter driving wheels. This class was primarily for heavy suburban work and the engines distinguished themselves on the services out of Paddington for many years. Collett even replaced the ageing o-4-2Ts with a new batch of ninety-five engines between 1932 and 1936; these were classified 4800. The 1930s also saw the appearance of the 5400 Class o-6-oPT with large 5 ft. 2 in. diameter driving wheels. This class was intended for use on those services which required an engine heavier than the o-4-2T but lighter than the 4500 Class 2-6-2T.

Churchward left the G.W.R. with a superb design of engine for every conceivable type of duty, and Collett's policy of continuing these, albeit in modified form, ensured their survival in basic form until the very end of steam. The British Railways' standard designs of the 1950s, which were desperately needed in many areas, were hardly required over the former G.W. network, due to Churchward's brilliant foresight half a century earlier, and the suburban, branch and cross country types were no exception to this rule.

SECTION 7

Mixed Traffic Engines

From the early days of main line operation, distinctions were made between locomotives for pulling passengers, as opposed to those for hauling freight. Some early engines did work all types of trains, but only circumstantially, and over sixty years were to elapse between the steam locomotive's inception and the advent of the mixed traffic locomotive proper.

The genesis occurred in 1866 when the first J15, 0-6-0 'Maids of all Work' were delivered to the Great Southern and Western Railway of Ireland. The same year, Sharp Stewart built an 0-4-2 'Mixed Traffic' engine for the Cambrian Railway. The appearance of Stroudley's D2 Class 0-4-2s in 1876 for the L.B. & S.C.R. hastened the concept and paved the way for Adam's famous 0-4-2 Jubilees which appeared on the L. & S.W.R. in 1887. The Jubilees were excellent 'all rounders' and appeared on many types of trains, and can be regarded as a late nineteenth century equivalent of the standard two-cylinder mixed traffic 4-6-0s of half a century later.

Several well known classes of inside-cylinder 0-6-0s were, in effect, mixed traffics, and Webb's L. & N.W.R. 18 in. Goods of 1880—known as 'Cauliflowers'—were frequently used on passenger trains, whilst Holden's GER, J15, 0-6-0s of 1883 were specifically intended as an all round design, as were his E4, 2-4-0 'Intermediates', with 5 ft. 8 in. diameter driving wheels, of 1891. Three years later an evolutionary milestone occurred, when the first two-cylinder mixed traffic 4-6-0s appeared on the Highland Railway with the famous Jones Goods. These were the first engines of this wheel arrangement to work in Britain, and despite their name, they were extensively used on passenger trains. Excellent as they were, they did little to pre-empt the general use 4-6-0 at that time. Many of these early all rounders tended to be random designs; the need for a mixed traffic engine was not so prevalent during the nineteenth century, and by 1900 the mixed traffic order had barely evolved.

At the turn of the century, Britain's locomotive builders were fully

occupied; delivery dates were long, and in response to the urgent need for more engines, eighty typically American 2–6–0 Moguls were imported from the U.S.A. for use on the Midland, Great Northern and newly formed Great Central Railways. The Mogul had long been established as a standard mixed traffic type in America, but good as these engines were, they had a short life, and many conservative railwaymen regarded their alien features as a 'Yankee intrusion'.

Nevertheless, the mixed traffic Mogul had appeared in Britain, and as part of the need to speed up freight services, Churchward introduced his 4300, 2–6–0 Moguls in 1911. These were similar to the American engines though slightly larger, and proved ideal for working medium sized goods trains at speed, and likewise semi-fast passenger trains. They created great interest and building continued until 1932.

The Mogul was, in effect, an 0–6–0 with a leading pony truck for stability at speed, and following the advent of higher boiler pressures and superheating, it remained the principal basis for the British mixed traffic engine until the 1930s, when it was largely superseded by the two-cylinder 4–6–0.

Within three years of Churchward producing his 4300s, Gresley's first Moguls appeared on the Great Northern. Known as 'Ragtimers', they fulfilled an urgent need for a fast goods engine, as such work had previously been unsatisfactorily performed by Ivatt's inside-cylinder 0–6–0s. The new engines performed excellently and helped to spread the mixed-traffic gospel. During World War One Maunsell introduced his N Class Moguls on to the South Eastern & Chatham Railway, followed by his U Moguls for the Southern. Both the N and U series formed an extremely effective section of the Southern's motive power, throughout that Company's existence. The Maunsell's Ns were followed in 1920 by Gresley's three-cylinder K3, 2–6–0s. These magnificent locomotives created new horizons in freight operation by their ability to run easily at speeds up to 70 mph with trains in excess of 600 tons in weight.

Southern Railway Maunsell S15 Class 4-6-0, No. 841 *Greene King* built in 1936 and preserved on the North Yorkshire Moors Railway. One of the most successful of the early mixed traffic 4-6-0s was the L. & S.W.R.'s S15s, first introduced by Urie in 1920. They had two cylinders and a driving wheel diameter of 5 ft. 7 in., and although originally intended for fast freight haulage, their proportions obviously rendered them suitable for passenger trains too. Building continued under Maunsell, and the last examples did not appear until 1936.

After the grouping, the L.M.S. was the only member of the Big Four without a stud of Moguls. This situation was effectively rectified in 1926, when the first of Hughes' 'Crabs' appeared, and by 1932, 245 were in operation. The Crabs spread to the entire L.M.S. system, and were especially distinctive with their large inclined cylinders, curved footplating and ornate chimney. As the definitive British Mogul, they were powerful and completely at home on all middle range duties.

Great Western Hall Class 4–6–0, No. 5900 *Hinderton Hall*, built in 1931 and preserved by the Great Western Society at Didcot. The prototype of this famous class appeared in 1924, when a Churchward 'Saint' express passenger 4–6–0 was rebuilt with 6 ft. diameter wheels. This engine was numbered 4900, and named *Saint Martin*. Building of the Halls proper commenced in 1928 with an improved version, and continued with further modifications, until 1950 to reach a total of 330 locomotives. The Halls were one of the stalwart mixed traffic 4–6–0s, and keenly contested by their admirers as being superior to the L.M.S. and L.N.E.R. equivalents, the Black 5s and B1s respectively.

Shortly after Stanier took office, he provided the L.M.S. with a class of new Moguls, identical in power to the Crabs but fitted with a taper boiler of very obvious Swindon derivation. Only forty were built, however, as the new engines served merely as a prelude to the Black 5 Mixed Traffic 4-6-os.

Although 4-6-os had been prevalent since the early years of the century, they were almost exclusively express passenger designs with large diameter driving wheels and often four cylinders. The mixed traffic 4-6-o evolved with only two cylinders and smaller driving wheels. These engines were a logical extension of the Mogul by having a bigger boiler and a leading bogie which not only helped to spread the extra weight, but gave better riding qualities when running.

Perhaps the true progenitor of the mixed traffic 4-6-o was Urie's H15s for the L. & S.W.R. This class appeared in 1914, and had two cylinders and 6 ft. o in. diameter driving wheels. Of equal significance, however, was an event which occurred ten years later, when a two-cylinder Great Western Saint was rebuilt with 6 ft. o in. diameter wheels to form a basis for the Hall Class which was built from 1928 right up until 1950. Another epic mixed traffic 4-6-o followed in 1934, when Stanier introduced the first of his Black 5s for the L.M.S. This was one of the most successful locomotives of all time and, as in the case of the Halls, building continued until 1950.

As the 1930s progressed, the mixed traffic 4-6-o was continued with the G.W.'s Granges and Manors, designed for lighter duties, but the next major class was Thompson's B1s which appeared in 1942 for the L.N.E.R. It was stated at the time that the B1s were intended to replace a plethora of ageing 4-6-os of various kinds, which totalled 387 engines of twenty-one different types! In fact, the utilitarian aspect of these new 4-6-os can be evidenced by the combined total of G.W. Halls, L.M.S. Black 5s and L.N.E.R. B1s being 1,682 engines.

The one significant deviation from this formula was Gresley's

Southern Railway Maunsell U Class 2-6-0, No. 1618 built in 1928 as one of the completely new engines based upon the rebuilt River 2-6-4Ts, and preserved on the Bluebell Railway. The origin of this mixed traffic Mogul lies in the River Class 2-6-4Ts, which originated on the South Eastern and Chatham Railway. The Rivers were suspected of being unstable at speed and from 1927 onwards they were rebuilt under Maunsell into 2-6-0 tender engines. They formed a useful class, and new building continued to the rebuilt tank design between 1928 and 1931, to reach a combined total of sixty engines.

three-cylinder V2, 2–6–2s of 1936. These were a shorter version of his A3 Pacifics, and the firebox spread out over the rear carrying wheels to give a grate area of 41 sq. ft. The result was a class of 184 superb engines which, apart from an amazing capacity for speed, performed phenomenal feats of haulage. From 1945 onwards, the V2s were often referred to as 'the engines which won the war'.

The post-war years saw the continuation of the Mogul for lighter

L.M.S. Black 5 4-6-0, No. 4767 *George Stephenson* built in 1947 and fitted with Stephenson's Link Motion, is preserved on the North Yorkshire Moors Railway. The Stanier Black 5 of 1934, one of the most successful locomotives in British history, was the definitive mixed traffic 4-6-0. Their two cylinders had an $18\frac{1}{2}$ in. diameter and 28 in. stroke; boiler pressure was 225 lbs, driving wheels 6 ft. diameter and tractive effort 25,455 lbs. Very economical and easy to maintain, they served on all types of work on the L.M.S. system. Some survived until 1968. Building ended in 1950, with 842 built, but they were effectively resurrected in the BR Standard 5, 73000 Class 4-6-0s of 1951.

mixed traffic work with Ivatt's 6400 and 3000 Classes for the L.M.S. These designs, along with Stanier's Black 5 and the Fairburn 2-6-4Ts were destined to have a fundamental place in steam's last testament— namely the British Railways' standard classes.

In these classes the evolution towards a mixed traffic concept became almost complete. The only exceptions were the solitary three-cylinder Pacific 'Duke of Gloucester'—which was intended to be the first of a new line of top link express engines—and the Class 9F 2-10-0 heavy mineral engine.

The 'Britannia' Pacifics and 73000 Class 4-6-0s both had 6 ft. 2 in. diameter driving wheels, and boiler pressures of 250 and 225 lbs per sq. in. respectively; these factors, combined with a fine balance of design, rendered them suitable for a wide range of fast passenger and freight work. The same all round suitability applied to the smaller designs; the 80000 Class 2-6-4Ts represented the climax of a long line of suburban designs, whilst the 76000 Class 2-6-0s upheld the great Mogul tradition. The 82000 Class 2-6-2Ts were, in essence, though not appearance, an updated version of Churchward's 4500 branch engines of 1906, whilst the 84000 push and pull fitted 2-6-2Ts, though based on Ivatt's L.M.S. 1200 Class, fulfilled the same niche as the

Left
L.N.E.R. Gresley K4 Class 2-6-0, No. 3442 *The Great Marquess* built in 1938 and preserved on the Severn Valley Railway. This class consisted of five potent Moguls which were introduced by Gresley for the West Highland line in 1937. Classified K4, they were the most powerful British Moguls with a tractive effort of 36,600 lbs. Although only moderate in size, the K4s had three-cylinders identical with those fitted on the larger K3, 2-6-0s. However, the K4 had been designed to produce short bursts of power when needed, and at low speed compared with the more continuous heavy demands made on main line engines such as the K3. In 1945, Thompson rebuilt a K4 into a two-cylinder engine and in so doing created a precedent for the seventy KI Class Moguls which were built under Peppercorn from 1949 onwards.

Lower Left
G.W.R. Manor Class 4-6-0, No. 7812 *Erlestoke Manor* built in 1939, and preserved on the Severn Valley Railway. No railway ever competed with the G.W.R.'s unfailing ability to produce efficient locomotives of standard designs for all levels of traffic. The Manor Class 4-6-0s were a slightly lighter version of the Granges, which in turn were a smaller version of the Halls. The Manors were designed by Collet for secondary lines where the heavier types were forbidden, especially the former Cambrian and Midland & South Western Junction Railway systems. The first twenty appeared in 1938-39 using wheels, motions and other parts from withdrawn 43XX Moguls. Another ten followed in 1950. Further building was cancelled in favour of the B.R. Standard designs.

Right
L.M.S. Ivatt 6400 Class 2-6-0, No. 46464 built in 1950 and preserved on the Strathspey Railway. The L.M.S.'s 6400 Class Moguls were introduced by Ivatt in 1946 to replace older classes on light services of all kinds. In common with his larger 3000 Class Moguls of the following year, the 6400's design was partly American inspired, both in labour saving devices and raised footplating; this latter aspect contrasted dramatically with the traditional British design. These American influences were partly the result of experiences gained with the S160 2-8-0s during World War Two. A total of 128 6400s was built up to 1952, and the engines spread far beyond the confines of the former L.M.S. system. After 1952 the 6400s were superseded by the very similar B.R. 78000, Class 2-6-0s.

Below
L.N.E.R. B1 Class 4-6-0, No. 1306 *Mayflower* built in 1948 and preserved on the Great Central Railway at Loughborough. Following Gresley's death in 1941, the L.N.E.R., under Thompson, adopted the 4-6-0 as the principal mixed traffic engine, and 310 B1s were put into traffic between 1942 and 1950. In common with the Black 5s, the B1s have no splashers over their driving wheels, but the two types differ considerably in firebox designs, the B1's being rounded as compared with the Black 5's Belpair type. The B1 was the exact equivalent of the L.M.S. Black 5, and was found throughout the entire L.N.E.R. system.

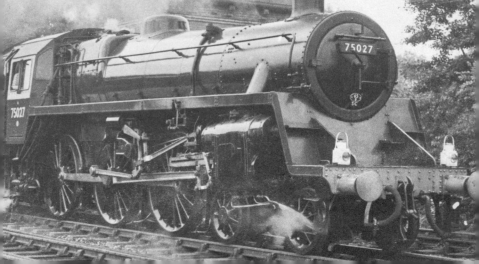

G.W.R.'s series of 5400 Class Pannier Tanks had during the 1930s.

It will be seen that through its evolution, the mixed traffic engine was only suitable for the middle range of duties—the older mixed traffic designs of inside cylinder 0-6-0 would have been just as unhappy on express passenger work as would the last Standard 5, 73000 Class 4-6-0s on heavy mineral hauling. If any broadly based mixed traffic design did emerge, it was the BR 9F 2-10-0s, which proved equally suitable working heavy main line expresses—on schedules of up to a mile a minute—as they were on heavy freight. Their nearest contender were the Britannias which undoubtedly showed an advantage on express work, but were greatly inferior in terms of heavy pulling. In addition, the 9F's $15\frac{1}{2}$ ton axle load, compared with the Britannia's $20\frac{1}{4}$ tons, gave it a far wider route availability for general work, and thus greater suitability as a mixed traffic engine. It is therefore a strange paradox that the one important design within the range of BR's standards which was not officially designated mixed traffic, was in actuality the finest example of mixed traffic evolution in the entire history of the British steam locomotive.

Had steam continued, it is highly probable that the two outer limits of top link express passenger and heavy freight would have come together into one common design. Perhaps this would have been a 2-8-2 or 4-6-4, visions of which had been glimpsed briefly by Gresley during the 1930s, but at that time any such aspirations had faded under the all pervading advance of the British Pacific.

Above Left
British Railway's Standard Britannia Class Pacific, No. 70013 *Oliver Cromwell* built in 1951 and preserved at Bressingham Steam Museum and Gardens. Possibly the best loved of B.R.'s standard designs, were the Britannia Class Pacifics of 1951. Their fine looks were matched by some excellent running, especially on the Great Eastern main line, where their best work was done. The Britannias were Britain's first two-cylinder Pacifics, and the first to be officially designated as mixed traffic engines. Furthermore, the Britannias, along with the 9F 2-10-0s, were the only two designs in the B.R. Standard range which were truly original and somewhat revolutionary designs.

Left
British Railway's Standard 4 Class 75000 4-6-0, No. 75027 built in 1954 and preserved on the Bluebell Railway. The B.R. Standard 4 Class 75000 appeared in 1951 as a smaller version of the Standard 5s for medium range duties. Their tractive-effort of 25,100 lbs was almost identical with the first G.W. Moguls of 1911, and only slightly less than the L.M.S. Crab 2-6-0s. However, as 4-6-0s, the Standard 4s had a lighter axle loading and greater flexibility for lively running. A total of eighty was built, the last appearing in 1957.

Index

Page numbers in *italics* refer to illustration captions.